THE HUMANITY
OF IT

KEVIN J. SMITH

The Anima Group

AUTHOR DEDICATION

To the talented and dedicated people of IT everywhere.

For my Julie.

ACKNOWLEDGMENTS

To the ever-changing and always-amazing people of IT with whom I am and have been so fortunate to work every day across many market-leading organizations globally. I look forward to traveling this journey with you over the next twenty-five years as we shape a new era for the IT organization and one that is built squarely upon our talented and dedicated people.

The professionals at Outskirts Press have been a joy to work with throughout the publishing process once again on this our fifth book together, and my thanks for holding to yet another aggressive schedule and bringing this new book to life.

My sincere thanks to those who made the IT Transformation Institute a reality—an organization much needed to bring a new and living framework of IT Transformation and Service Management best practices to the countless IT organizations globally in search of a better future and a smarter way of working.

PREFACE

The remarkable and accelerating advancements of technology in the past ten years, including the likes of Artificial Intelligence (AI), Robotics, and Automation, have caused us to rethink virtually everything in the world of Information Technology (IT) today.

While we naturally focus on the technology itself, there is a far bigger and more compelling issue here related to people—the wonderful humanity of IT. Herein lies a vital and exciting story that needs to be addressed, because at the core of this issue is the essence of the future of IT. Equally important is the link humanity holds to the future of virtually every business. This simple and fascinating story is what we will focus on throughout the book.

The story that follows is the essential and irreplaceable role our people will play in the future survival and then the success of the IT organization and of the business.

It has become increasingly clear that the future of IT is not what many people would have us believe. In the many stories related to technology and a new generation of intelligent technology, what is often lost is the vital role the people of IT will play in the future of this organization and, in particular, the critical next decade of IT during which a never-before-seen shift will occur in IT and how the business operates every day.

Simply acquiring and deploying the latest technology is not enough and will not guarantee success. If anything, the rapid deployment of technology in the next decade in the absence of a technology strategy and, more importantly, a strategy around how the IT organization will thoughtfully leverage our people can result in a slowing of the business and ultimately failure.

It is our people and priceless diversity of humanity that is uniquely capable of making technology strategic to the business.

What we must appreciate as IT professionals is that the strategic force that will drive IT into the future is not simply the technology itself, regardless of its power and seeming sophistication. It's all about the talented people of IT and their ability to delegate volumes of work to technology and therein create a new opportunity to transition our uniquely skilled and experienced people into more strategic roles—and roles that are closer to the market and to our customers. This distinction is so important.

The ability of technology to provide a helping hand in moving our people into more dynamic roles and closer to the customer is a key consideration we will explore. Taking this a step further, humanity is also uniquely capable of lifting up technology and making it even better. Yes, surprising to many, technology needs humanity more than our people need the new generation of intelligent technology. What we will explore are some unlikely but vital elements of this new relationship between technology and our people, including a new shape of partnership that now becomes possible for the first time—a fascinating and necessary mentoring model that will emerge, a new culture that will take shape to bring out the best of technology and our people, a new definition of the workday as being driven and enabled by technology and the fundamental need to renew our focus on and passion for the customer.

What we will discover is that technology is uniquely able to unlock new ways of working and new levels of productivity while at the same time bringing us back to what is so vital to our future—a focus on the wonderful people of IT and of the business and the renewed search for how we better serve our customers.

When deployed effectively and strategically, technology en-ables any business to better deliver a service or product to our customers.

I felt it was important to write the book at this time and on this topic because the wonderful people of IT have not received the attention needed and earned. Technology continues to evolve at a dizzying rate, all the while grabbing the attention of the market, press, and social media. Collectively, the view of our world today is shaped by these channels, and everybody loves to talk about technology. Yes, it's easy to focus on the compelling potential of AI and Robotics, to name a couple of the stars of technology, but this misses the point.

There is a far bigger story here.

Technology is not reducing the value of people—the truth is very different.

Technology is now able to up-value our people and bring atten-tion to the true miracle of humanity and our people's unique and priceless skills.

These skills now become better understood and more valued and, with this, far more appreciated. Then, with this appreciation we will be able to more strategically leverage humanity in order to el-evate the performance of IT and elevate the performance of the full business. This is essentially a chain of performance and value that is vital to the future of business success everywhere and uniquely enabled by the new partnership of humanity and technology.

*Only through the miracle of humanity
can we find the true future of IT*

TABLE OF CONTENTS

CHAPTER 1

THE RISE OF PEOPLE

The accelerating evolution of technology and that of our people are inextricably linked. As technology improves, and it certainly has dramatically in the past decade, we have begun to appreciate a remarkable phenomenon that many did not anticipate—the ascension and evolution of our people.

People are wonderful and limitless in their unique talents and abilities.

Technology has done something not thought possible previously, and that is the lifting-up of our people in ways that only technology could. What people can and will do for people is limited. Technology was needed at this time but not for the sake of technology or the abilities of technology itself. The new generation of intelligent technology was needed at this time to provide leverage to our people just when the miracle of humanity was needed in business and in our culture more than ever.

Technology has and will now bring our people into focus and elevate our people into more focused and more strategic roles across IT and the business.

The thirty-year history of IT has in many ways placed a weight on the shoulders of our talented people and blocked them from occupying the roles where they are needed the most. The operational legacy of IT has created barriers to the strategic promotion of our people as it has been our people who worked long hours every day to support the daily demands of operating IT and the business. This is very much a challenge of our own making. In the traditional model of IT, technology was not able to effectively and consistently offload our people in a way that freed up significant time and enabled IT leadership to shift the right people onto other work that demanded the unique skills and experience of the human touch.

This strategic shift is now possible because AI, robotics, and automation have improved to the point where many high-volume, repetitive, and well-defined tasks can be delegated to intelligent technology, thereby creating an exciting opportunity to refocus some of our people onto more impactful and strategic work.

This shift will prove to have a dramatic and lasting impact on the IT organization and across the business. Although we will explore the more complete set of tasks in the coming pages, a few good examples include:

Innovation

Building relationships

Strategic partnerships

Customer success

Creative projects

Superior communications

Improving speed and agility

Mentoring junior staff

All these activities are strategic to the future of the business and

uniquely require the skills and experience of our people.

While we can likely agree that each of these is important, even critical, the fact is that the operational demands of the IT organization, along with the lack of resources and precious time, have severely limited our ability to invest in these activities in the past.

Today, that has changed for the first time. Technology now lends a helping hand to IT and to the business at precisely the right time in order to enable leadership to move the right people onto these strategic activities. It is not simply a matter of an all-or-nothing allocation of time to these tasks because that is not practical today for most organizations. Some operational responsibilities will be required of our most talented and experienced people.

The details of exactly how and how quickly we begin to make this shift would be missing the point entirely. What can't be lost here is that for over thirty years the IT organization has held the desire and the dream to become more strategic, to be better aligned with the business, and to act more proactively. But the reality of daily life in the IT organization was very different. The many daily escalations, tactical projects, lack of staff, and operational needs forced IT to live hand-to-mouth and blocked our ability to make this shift.

But today, with the help of intelligent technology, we are able to begin making this shift, and it will change everything.

It is not unreasonable to assume that up to 90% of daily work in IT will be automated over the next five years.

I document this shift as described by the 90/90 Rule in my book *The IT Imperative*. This is not a crazy dream; it is a reality for most IT organizations and made possible by a new generation of AI and Automation tools.

Imagine the opportunity this creates across IT and the business as we are able to offload the majority of high-volume and repetitive tasks that have placed such an enormous weight on the people of IT for decades. This shift will change the manner in which IT works, how IT works with the business, and that is just the beginning. There are so many other benefits in motion here, including improved retention of IT staff, the creation of new jobs in the IT organization, enhanced compensation plans, the desire of young talented workers to pursue a career in IT, and much more. We will explore the inner workings of this shift throughout the pages of the following chapter and throughout the book.

PEOPLE MAKE TECHNOLOGY BETTER

There is another important but not commonly understood dynamic around the relationship between technology and people. Yes, we will frequently discuss how technology can offload and assist our people in the daily performance of the many tasks and business processes that represent the motion of the IT organization and the business. This is an easy one.

But what we might lose sight of is the important need that is growing within every business today—the fundamental requirement of technology to be enhanced and enriched by our people.

This improvement can take many forms, including:

Capturing key decision-making rules

Modeling business rules and workflows

Describing priority definitions

Providing context for business processes

Providing customer-related content

Describing exceptions to standard rules

Each of these examples extends the capabilities of technology and at the same time ensures technology can be more useful and more strategic in the future. Technology can only advance so far on the merits of technology itself. This human assist we are providing to technology benefits technology immediately in that we are ensuring intelligent technology is more useful and more impactful to both IT and to the business. But the benefit of this human partnership goes much further. It then enables technology to become a more capable partner to our people and to further offload the tactical and well-defined tasks that have occupied so much of our people's time and capacity for the past thirty years.

This human enrichment of technology enables technology to rise up and be a better and more capable partner to humanity.

This cycle then further accelerates our ability to move our talented and experienced people on to more strategic, more creative, innovative, and customer-facing activities. Each of these activities is both strategic to IT and to the business and capable of improving the performance of virtually every element of the business. The value that is created here is virtually unlimited.

This process of humanity enriching technology will also serve as a much-needed reminder of the remarkably rich and diverse talents of our people. Of course we understand this at some level, but in most cases this appreciation is not active and lives somewhere outside our daily thoughts. But when we begin to automate work and tasks and business processes, we are forced to itemize and capture these rich and advanced skills.

THE SKILLS OF HUMANITY

People are remarkable.

They are the most advanced physical machine and the most capable thinking machine ever created in our history. And every person is perfectly unique.

Technology will continue to improve into the foreseeable future, and as it does, it will serve to constantly remind us not of the capabilities of technology, but of the wonderful and limitless skills possessed by our people.

Taken for granted for many years, these skills are the key to the future of IT and of the business and all with good reason.

A few of the skills that are unique to humanity and for which our understanding and assignment of value will grow in the decade ahead include:

Empathy

Sense of humor

Complex problem-solving

Relationship building

Intuition

Passion

Leadership

Charisma

Verbal communication

Natural negotiating skills

A limitless range of emotions

Each of these talents is remarkable in its own right, and this is just the beginning. The accelerated development of technology will bring into focus our understanding of what intelligent technology is qualified to do in IT and in the business today. At the same time, it will usher in a new era of appreciating the advanced skills of humanity. This appreciation then immediately creates a dialogue around how we can best leverage the abilities of technology while at the same time leveraging the unique skills of humanity.

Figure 1.1 The Remarkable Skills of Humanity

This is good for the IT organization in that it will enable us to improve the overall performance and speed of IT. Further, this stronger model for IT is coming at the perfect time, a time when virtually every business needs improved innovation, faster velocity of delivered services and products, and a superior customer experience.

Think about this carefully for a moment. The only possible success with meeting these goals is through the IT organization due to our widespread dependency on technology and even more, the strategic role of technology in the future.

IT is uniquely capable of understanding and delivering to this need. Further, when we embrace this mission and accept this responsibility, it becomes clear quickly that intelligent technology plays a key role in delivering to this vision. Then we immediately recognize that humanity must work alongside technology to deliver the unique skill that our people possess today but have been limited due to the tactical and operational demands placed on the collective back of IT every day.

Every IT organization must understand that our only path forward to business success is deploying intelligent technology in the right roles and then leveraging the remarkable talents of humanity alongside this powerful technology.

Having only one of these two pieces will not do—it must be the best technology and our best people working side by side.

With this model in place, anything becomes possible.

PEOPLE ARE NOW STRATEGIC

Perhaps there is no greater development related to the improvement of technology across the IT organization than that of moving our people into more strategic roles. Even with the remarkable advancements of technology over the past ten years, people are uniquely able to perform the strategic work of today that requires our attention.

Long a dream of the IT organization and IT leadership, this goal of moving our people onto strategic work now becomes reality. For the first time, IT is able to assign a growing percentage of the daily work in IT to intelligent technology, thereby enabling us to gain some time back in each day to ensure our people are ready. Capable technology can offload our people and create the precious time that has been all but impossible to recover in the course of our day. We have tried in vain to find this time for the past thirty years, and this time savings is now possible. With that yoke of the daily tactical, operational, and repetitive work lifted from our people, we can move them on to more strategic initiatives.

We will discuss these initiatives repeatedly throughout the book, but a few examples are:

Innovation

Customer-facing work

Improved communications

Improved customer relationships

Business engagement and outreach

Developing new metrics

Mentoring

Improving the user experience

And much, much more.

This needed and long overdue shift of people onto strategic work will bring us many benefits, not the least of which will be the showcasing of the unique skills and talents of our people that have for too long been obscured by the highly repetitive and operational work that has demanded our time for decades.

Our people will truly shine when focused on the work that requires creative problem-solving, communications, relationship building, new and unconventional ideas, and related activities that tap into the unique and very human skills of our people.

This line of thinking brings us back to technology, our ally in this important partnership, and the delegation of the structured and well-defined work that technology can take on going forward.

It won't be hard for us to identify this work—we simply take inventory of the most commonly performed tasks and business processes across the IT organization. It's important to start with the high-volume work because it represents the best opportunity to save time for our people. This is the very work that is likely taking so much time from our people. With these high-volume tasks and business processes identified and listed, we then look at the degree to which each of these work items is structured, consistent, and well-defined. These characteristics make the work a good candidate for automation and the leveraging of new-generation AI capabilities.

To summarize, the work we will automate over the next five years (through the year 2025) as a delegation exercise from people to technology will have the following profile:

Operational in nature

High volume

Well-defined and structured

Well-established decision criteria and business rules

Mature

Static in nature—not currently undergoing dynamic changes

Inherently repeatable

Exhibits a linear workflow process

We should recognize that this profile accomplishes a couple of things, helping to ensure the technology can be successful in automating the work itself, and the volume of work is sufficient to offload the time necessary for our people to shift their attention to the strategic initiatives we discussed earlier. Both of these considerations are important and both put technology and our people in a position to be successful. This is a critical distinction—both technology and our people must be successful and productive in their respective roles in order for the partnership model to be prosperous for the IT organization and for the business. This choice of language is not an accident. We must all care about putting technology in a position to be successful just as we care about our people being successful.

Never forget this relationship—with a successful application of technology, we create the opportunity for a person, or a team of people, to be equally successful and potentially even more so. As with any successful partnership, the parties lift one another to new heights.

PEOPLE CREATE A NEW ERA FOR IT

Many people have assumed that new, powerful, and intelligent technologies will usher in a new era for IT. While it is not difficult to see how one might take this position, I see it a bit differently. My increasingly resolute view is that there is a new generation of the IT organization rapidly forming around us every day, and we must together embrace this idea of a new and fundamentally different IT. The primary driver for this new generation in IT is our people—the talented and dedicated people of IT.

As an interesting element of the forces driving this new generation, technology has a role and a very important role at that. Our people, for many years capable of creating this new era of IT, have been unable to do so due to the overwhelming amount of tactical and operational work that has blocked them from the leadership and innovation activities that will so strongly influence the future direction of the IT organization and the business.

Today, with more capable, intelligent technology—including AI, Robotics, and Automation—readily available to our IT professionals, we can delegate a significant volume of the tactical work to this technology and then reassign some IT staff to more strategic initiatives. This seems simple enough, but the shift is possible now for the first time in the long history of the IT organization.

This delegation is not intended to downplay the wonderful capabilities of technology, because that is not the intent—the power of intelligent technology today is immense, but simply not evolved to the point of being able to match the unique abilities of our talented people. And, in fairness to the technology, it is superior to humanity in specific areas, so this serves as another reminder that our goal here is to leverage the best of both people and technology and improve the overall performance of the IT organization, while putting our people into a position to be at their best every day.

Powerful technology working in harmony with our people is an unstoppable force for the future of IT and what we refer to in the section title as a "New Era" for every element of the IT organization. In turn this will create a new era for the business. This point is important and one that we will make throughout the book: the dependence of the business has grown to the extent that as goes the IT organization, so goes the business. The fate of the organization is now inextricably linked to that of the IT organization due to the deeply rooted reliance on technology, systems, and data. It is simply not possible for the modern business to compete and to be successful in the global marketplace without an ability to leverage technology in a manner that complements the corporate strategy.

This might all seem like common sense, but the separation of technology and the business was possible in the past, as recently as just five to ten years ago, and that is no longer the case. We can find reminders of this every day as we see businesses fail, many of which were thriving organizations, even market leaders, just ten to fifteen years ago, and

because these now threatened or failed businesses were simply unable to find the right role for the mighty Triune of tools, systems, and data.

It all happens so fast.

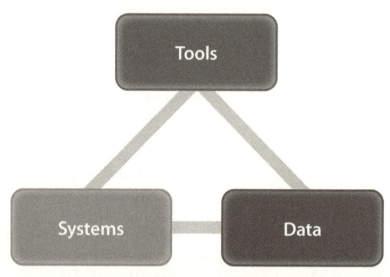

Figure 1.2 The Triune of Technology

When the pairing of technology and people is executed well, in-cluding both the operational roles and the synergies with the over-all business strategy, it is a remarkable thing to behold. This unique combination becomes the genesis of the new era of IT and what can be called a new era for the organization—one that is only made possible through the elevation of people, which in turn was made possible by a new generation of intelligent technology. All of the elements are woven together in a way that is precious to the orga-nization in countless ways.

While our focus will be on many of the details of how we are plac-ing technology into the right roles across the business while at the same time thoughtfully moving our people into the more creative and strategy-oriented roles, this shift will create a foundation for the future that will bring countless benefits to us for decades to come.

Just a few of the broad benefits we will begin to see in the years ahead:

Improved customer satisfaction

Growth in the Innovation pipeline

Improved tenure in the IT organization

Higher customer renewal rates

Higher sales success rates

Improved user experiences

Superior communications across the IT organization

Successful partnering with the business

It is recommended that we establish new success metrics for the next decade of IT, and these metrics need not incorporate all these examples, but they should include a few that make sense for a particular business type and industry. These metrics then connect our daily actions to the strategy and goals of the IT organization and enable our people to stay focused on results—not just on results that might reflect past priorities but the results that will carry IT into the next decade of change.

While there is an increasing amount of evidence that humanity will lead and shape the new era for IT, the thoughtful leveraging of technology will launch the chain of events that will bring our people into the position to lead and think in new ways, which is long overdue. Technology is now so much more capable, and learning at a faster rate than ever, that it enables the organization to lift the burden of work product that has blocked our people from the shrugging-off of operational work for decades.

This simple but remarkable shift, this inflection for IT, is precisely what will carry us into the new era that will fundamentally change how IT thinks and acts every day. And this change will have an equally dramatic and lasting impact on the business.

Soon, it will be hard to imagine the previous model and how we survived the brute-force lifestyle for over thirty years.

CHAPTER 2

A NEW IT CULTURE

Humanity is uniquely capable of creating culture, and then in the right culture, our people can thrive. A new and necessary culture is now upon us. We must take the responsibility to focus on this dimension of IT and never assume that the right culture will somehow just happen. What might look natural and effortless from the outside is anything but. Any thriving and vibrant culture took careful and thoughtful planning and the commitment of a few people and ultimately modeled the right behavior and the right plans and drew other people into the cause.

Passion is contagious, and where we find authentic passion we will often find optimism. This is something we all want to be part of. Passion draws us in. Invariably, optimism creates confidence, and confidence more often than not results in success, and we have then crafted an unstoppable force that generates so much more.

Culture must be shaped by a strategy, made a priority, and have the benefit of resources and teams assigned to cultural initiatives in order to make sure we are moving forward, although sometimes slowly, in order to get it right. It seems to be such a simple thing, but often culture is not a priority in IT. It's just not something we have traditionally focused on or put resources behind.

Fortunately, that is now changing. The best IT organizations understand that culture is a powerful force in the future of IT and to not invest in culture, to not make a new culture a priority, is to all but ensure the organization will struggle or fail outright.

It is fair to say that in the right culture, our people grow and often exceed our greatest expectations, but in a stale and stagnant culture, even our best people will cease to grow, and in many cases will choose to leave the organization in search of something better and more fulfilling. So, it falls to us to ensure that culture is a priority for now and far into the future in order to ensure we accomplish the following basic and essential goals for the wonderful Humanity of IT:

Create an environment for personal growth

Provide for long-term career development

Have some fun and enjoy the journey

Encourage passion in all we do

Cultivate innovation

Build a sense of Team

Establish a new and effective communications model

Recognize and reward contributions

Focus on quality of life for all staff members

Make no mistake that all these powerful things are uniquely created through a healthy culture and are all but impossible in the wrong culture.

What we see in the traditional culture of the IT organizations is all too often a failure to create a plan for growth and personal development, along with a failure to reward key contributions. This results in the loss of the very people who are our future.

These people are the talented and dedicated workers who have the skills, emotional makeup, and mindset that are so important to the future of a transformed IT organization. What we desperately need is the simultaneous development of the people we have in IT today and to recruit and attract new staff members who represent all the things so important to building a vibrant and energized IT organization for the future.

Remember, the people we have in the IT organization today are equally as valuable as the new hires we might make in the future. This is where our focus must begin. If anything, the workers in the IT organization of today should be our top priority because they are with us now, ready today, capable of making a difference now. And even a small investment in our current people can bring us a large and lasting payback. Our current people will immediately recognize a commitment to an improved culture and will want to be part of this critical renovation of the fabric of how we work every day. This natural desire should be recognized. In most cases we should make our current staff members a part of the launch of the teams or task forces we will soon form to create an elevated sense of focus on culture and to put some structure around the changes and improvements we must make. We simply can't assume this will all just happen as the result of discussion and a new sense of priority. It is necessary to assign people to a culture-focused team or teams, to empower the team to drive change, and to put incentives in place in order to reward the team when real change comes.

The very best IT organizations, those that have seen real cultural change and dramatically improved IT performance, have followed this simple formula:

1. Announce and consistently reinforce a new commitment to culture.
2. Form a team or task force to focus on cultural change and improvements.

3. Select a passionate and diverse group of people for the team.
4. Define clear cultural goals in cooperation with the team.
5. Provide reasonable financial incentives to members of the team when goals are met.

Yes, much of this is simply good common sense but often missing when IT organizations take on a new focus on culture. Follow this simple outline and success is much more likely to come.

I recommend this as a good next step in driving our culture forward—the formation of a few small teams or a broader task force that will have the support of IT leadership and will have the responsibility for rallying our organization around the Culture initiative along with the necessary commitment to timelines, deliverables, and resources.

COMMUNICATION

Improving the culture of IT must include improved communication every day.

This is not an option.

With that said, we should also recognize this won't be easy and in many ways cuts against the traditional grain of the historical IT culture. Communicating was not natural for IT as well as not a priority and so it became an element of the daily IT rhythm we were not good at performing. The coordination of the day-in and day-out workings of the IT organization simply did not include a focus on communications. And with that lack of focus, communicating was something we just didn't do very well and accepted as "not really an IT thing."

Sound familiar?

Let's be clear that although this might have been common for the IT of the past, this is not an indication of what we are capable of. There is a big difference between haven't and can't, my friends. That brings us back to the untapped talents of our people in IT. I'm convinced, both due to a belief in the capabilities of our people and having seen this change happen on several occasions, that with some focus and attention, we can transform the average IT organization into one that communicates very effectively.

No longer can we use the excuse that we just aren't very good at communicating; there is too much at stake here. In the beginning we will focus on improved communications within the IT organization and then with an improved model in place, we will turn our attention to improving the quality and cadence of communications between IT and the business as well as between and IT and our customers. As with many other things we will discuss throughout the book, we will discover that once we begin to make improvements, in this case with communications, we are forming good habits. And the good continues to grow—an unstoppable force of influence. It becomes just what we do every day and no longer requires a conscious and unnatural effort.

Assuming most of you will agree that we need to be better at communicating in the IT organization every day, we need to recognize up front that the model we build must be one we can live with. It must be a communications model that is not painful, that is not impractical. If with a little thoughtful design we can create a model that is more natural, easier to live with, and yet still effective then that can be something we can commit to and people will rally around.

The good news is that the parameters of this model are better understood today, and the model works very well when put into action.

The framework of a new communications model looks something like this:

Informal

Quick and easy exchanges and updates

Frequent

Inexpensive

Natural

Painless

Fast

Unstructured

Adaptable

Utilizes existing tools and verbal updates

Note this model is not too unlike the communication model used commonly outside the workplace today. Think in terms of tools like text and chat. Social media would be another example.

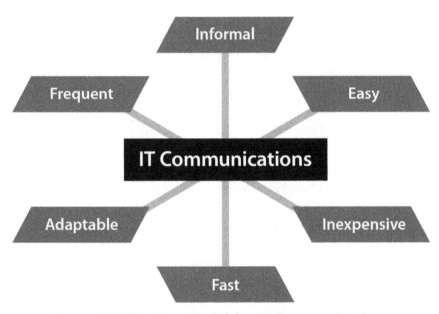

Figure 2.1 The New Model for IT Communications

Communications in the past of the IT organization created many challenges because the model was more formal, more structured, less frequent, and often utilized reporting tools and formal presentations. This model was painful and slow and required a great deal of time to create the updates, a model that was very unnatural for our people. And so it becomes not hard to understand why it was not successful.

With the rise of social media and the simultaneous increased use of smart phones and mobile devices,

a very different communications model has emerged in how we communicate with family and friends, and it only makes sense to leverage this model in the workplace.

This model is simple, natural, fast, and fun. Exactly what we need for the culture of IT: a new and fresh start to how we communicate.

It would be a big mistake to assume that these characteristics of fast and simple would result in something that would be ill-suited to the workplace and unprofessional. That is absolutely not the case. In fact, we could make the argument that this model is more effective and more suited to the business of the future than the model of the past.

Some of the best IT organizations today are using this model every day, and it has proven to be very effective and well received by the IT staff. Expanding on this point a bit, a couple of examples of specific methods that have worked well include:

> *Daily team huddles that last 10-15 min.*

> *Team/organization chat platforms*

> *SMS groups*

> *Short weekly team updates over voice/video calls*

This model works very well and can be adapted as necessary to the organization and the current state of the business.

A culture simply won't improve without a commitment to improved communication, so let's get started now.

INNOVATION AS LIFESTYLE

The winners in the new global marketplace, virtually without exception, will be innovators. Innovation is highly coveted by customers in every marketplace. Innovation is exciting and has the ability to change our life as innovation can both attract new customers to a business and build a sense of loyalty for existing customers. Although it is easy to think of innovation examples in consumer electronics, smartphones and automobiles for example (Apple and Tesla come to mind), innovation is happening in every market and will reshape how we live and how we work in the decades to come.

It can also be said that those organizations that failed to innovate in the past ten to twenty years are those organizations that have failed or are now threatened with extinction. Companies like Toys-R-Us and Sears are good examples of cultures that for many reasons were unwilling or unable to adapt to a new set of standards in the marketplace, a new consumer with new expectations, and a new digital and mobile economy. The marketplace is simultaneously unforgiving and generous in its reward for those companies that advance product and services innovations.

Although a few of the new market leaders have been identified over the past ten years, most will emerge in the decade ahead, and so there lies before us a tremendous opportunity for those organizations willing to make a lasting commitment to innovation.

Innovation is not some mysterious, magical, and hidden process that occurs behind closed doors. Innovation is about creating the right environment and then doing the hard work day after day. Innovation is about commitment, and a willingness to take chances.

Innovation can only grow in a fertile culture that values the process of innovation.

There is no single formula for innovation, but a few common characteristics of an organization that is prepared to successfully innovate include:

>*Leadership commitment to innovation*
>
>*Forums that encourage the exchange of new ideas*
>
>*A mechanism to explore and prove raw concepts*
>
>*The recognition and reward for new and creative ideas*
>
>*The commitment of time and resources to the innovation engine*
>
>*A culture that is tolerant of some risk-taking*
>
>*An organization that is willing to explore new things in every form*
>
>*A culture that actively nurtures and attracts diverse skillsets*
>
>*The mobilization of small teams to pursue innovation initiatives*

No doubt you can add a few items to this list if you have been part of successful innovation, but this gives us an outline to get started.

From this we can take a number of cultural priorities that must be considered when we plan and shape the new culture for IT. Innovation initiatives must be a key element of the plan and then we develop the daily cadence of the work that occurs across the IT organization. This includes a consistent and visible effort in support of innovation.

This commitment to innovation won't be easy in the beginning. But it's important enough to make the investment and to make the shift in priorities and resource allocation that gives innovation a chance to happen.

People are naturally drawn to innovation because it's a fundamentally creative process, a process that is fun and exciting.

This process also naturally attracts our best thinkers, the people with creative and big-idea talents. These are precisely the people we want and need to be part of innovation.

Then, after we make these big changes and these smaller shifts to nurture innovation, we begin to see it happen more naturally, and it becomes part of our lifestyle. It is no longer something that requires a conscious effort.

We just make time every day for innovation, and the great ideas begin to blossom into the innovations of the future. This innovation lifestyle then begins to bring us many benefits beyond the fruits of the innovations themselves. Innovation initiatives help to retain our best people and help to attract the talented people we need to bring into the IT organization for the future.

The commitment to innovation pays back to us in so many visible and just as many less visible ways. This commitment then builds momentum, and this momentum makes innovation a bit easier, more natural, and woven into the daily thinking and work that occurs across the IT organization every day.

DIVERSITY

Simply put, diversity has not been a strength of the IT organization or, as such, of the IT culture over the past forty years. The reasons for this are many, but we won't take the time here to explore those reasons and instead will focus on solutions and the need for positive change in the future.

Diversity of our people sows the changes we need in our culture and how we think. Diversity makes us stronger and enables us to work differently.

Key IT initiatives for the future—communications, innovation, new skills, business outreach, leveraging intelligent technology, building new relationships, moving closer to the customer, and many more—will all demand that we build a more diverse workforce and a more diverse culture for the future of IT. We simply can't meet these challenges with the same workers with the same skills toiling away immersed in the same culture. Preserving this traditional model for the IT organization would almost certainly result in our inability to meet these new challenges, a failure in the IT organization, and a failure for the business to meet the new challenges of the new global marketplace.

Conversely, with a new and more diverse set of skills and a more diverse organization of people, anything becomes possible for the IT organization committed to building an organization that embraces this new model.

Diversity has many dimensions, including:

Diversity of skills

Ethnic diversity

Age diversity

A stronger presence of women

Diversity of work experience

Diversity of culture

Diversity of education

Diversity of personal interests

You get the idea. Making a concerted effort to build a culture for IT that embraces this diversity, that seeks out this diversity, and celebrates this diversity directly contributes to the future capabilities of the IT organization and as such directly enables the future success of both tactical and strategic initiatives. Meaning that this diversity enables us to complete our daily work better and to staff and drive successful strategic initiatives as well.

This balance is important—better at the small but important things and also better at delivering strategic successes and transforming IT into an organization that leads the business.

Yes, this is ambitious, but this is our future and all but impossible with the same people and the same skills and the same thinking we've had for the past four decades in IT. We can only rebuild the culture of IT and transform the IT organization with a more diverse and energized set of teams who believe anything is possible and have an authentic passion for the work we do across IT every day.

This is not intended to imply that we must rid ourselves of the people currently in the IT organization—that is certainly not the case. What we must do is develop diversity, including diverse skills within the people we have today, and at the same time we must make transfers into the IT organization, backfilling positions where possible, and the hiring of new positions (not common but it will happen) shaped by a new priority around diversity. We elevate the emphasis on the diversity elements we listed earlier, and with each upskilled, cross-trained, and new hire we make the IT organization stronger. This is another case of balance in that we are both developing new skills in our existing people, emphasizing new initiatives with our current people, attracting new people into IT from other organizations, and on a parallel and equally urgent path seeking a new and broader profile for new hires. This is all within our control. We must focus on one step at a time, one person at a time, and with these small steps, we begin to make a real difference in the IT organization and our Culture.

We're also sending a message to the IT organization and to the business that diversity is important, and we are building a new culture filled with new talents for the future. Of course, this is much more than meets the eye at work here. A more diverse culture also means a more dynamic, healthy, capable, and a more resilient culture. We are crafting an IT organization that will work differently, make decisions differently, and produce superior results. A culture that is capable of driving strategic initiatives, yes, but also of completing the day-to-day work that remains important and completing this operational work and tactical projects more effectively.

With diversity and only with a diverse culture are we able to do everything we could do before and do it even better. At the same time IT is now able to drive more proactive and strategic engagements more effectively where this was simply not possible previously.

SIMPLE IS BETTER

Simplicity is remarkable.

Never underestimate simple.

Simplicity is difficult to fully appreciate in its ability to transform an organization, the culture, and the work that is performed every day. Simple can be an unequaled force of superior performance in our systems and tools.

A few natural benefits of simple:

Simple solutions are more reliable.

Simple systems scale better.

Simple systems are more repeatable.

Simplified systems are less costly to maintain.

Simple systems scale better.

Simple systems are more agile.

Simple systems resist failure better.

Simple systems are easier to understand.

Simple systems are more inherently trainable.

Simple solutions are faster.

And this is just the beginning of the rich and surprising value of simplicity.

When we take on the goal of simplicity in all we do, it begins to influence our culture in many ways, both expected and unexpected. Simplicity brings us short-term benefits and long-term value with a virtually unlimited ceiling of growth.

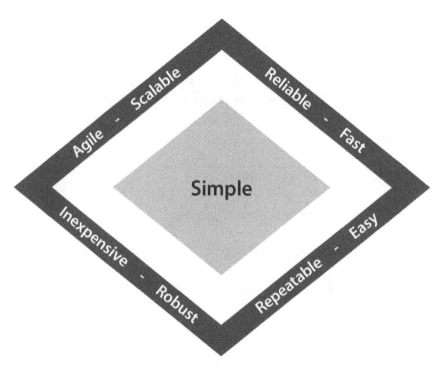

Figure 2.2 The Power of Simple

The goal of simplicity will change how we look at all existing tools, application, technologies, systems, and solutions. It will also change how we work every day in performing the necessary tasks and business processes that are the fabric of daily IT operations. This is just the normal work that happens every day. Recognize that much of this work has been in place for decades, in some cases for twenty to thirty years, so some level of inspection is long overdue.

In keeping with our theme of simplicity, the best way to inspect these efforts is with a simple set of questions and reflections. These questions can be applied to the work that we perform and to the tools, applications, and systems that make up the IT portfolio. You will notice that these questions are basic stuff, common sense in most cases, and that is exactly as it should be.

A few sample questions that will help us simplify our daily work:

> *Is this work necessary?*
>
> *What value is this work providing and has that value been verified recently?*
>
> *Can any part of this work be eliminated?*
>
> *Can we accomplish the same result with less effort?*
>
> *What steps in this process can we simplify?*
>
> *How can we complete this work faster?*
>
> *What element of this work is not repeatable and how can we make it more so?*
>
> *Can this work be automated?*
>
> *Is any element of this work confusing or complex?*
>
> *If so, why is the complexity required or can it be eliminated/ simplified?*

This list is intended to get you started; feel free to add other questions that are appropriate for your organization and industry.

A few assumptions to keep in mind—nothing should be off-limits, asking questions is a good thing, being curious is a great thing, and brainstorming better solutions with teammates will often result in us finding a better way to work.

Taking a few minutes to think is a great habit to develop for the future. Too often the people of the IT organization are a step behind the business and just trying to survive the day. Just trying to get the work of today done will all but ensure that tomorrow looks just like today, and we can't afford that lifestyle. Especially now with so much change in the world around us and with so much change happening in the business.

A few sample questions that will help us simplify our tools and systems:

If a legacy solution, is this system/application necessary today?

Has the need for the legacy system/application been verified recently?

What measurable value is it providing to IT and to the business?

What is the cost to maintain the system/application?

Has the system/application had reliability issues in the past?

Has the system/application had performance issues in the past?

How can we make this system/application less costly and easier to maintain?

Do we have another system/application that can perform the same function(s)?

How effectively does this system/application scale?

How quickly and effectively are changes possible in the system/application?

Are there components of the system/application that are considered complex or inflexible?

If so, how can these components be simplified or replaced?

Remember, asking questions is good, digging for facts is good, and searching for a simpler way to work is great. Nothing is off-limits, and all questions are good questions.

We are trying to build reliable, repeatable, scalable, and agile solutions, so all the systems and applications in place today must be held to this standard. This is not intended to imply that we should conduct an immediate and reckless housecleaning. That is not possible or practical. What it does mean is that we need to review, over a reasonable window of time, every system and application in place today, recognizing these systems have not been audited or reviewed in many years if ever, with a focus on simplicity and making these systems better prepared for the future and more cost effective. The standards of reliable, repeatable, scalable, fast, and agile should be reinforced at all times, at every step.

A final comment on this topic: in many cases the most effective strategy to achieve the results we are seeking here is through a commitment to simplification in all that we are doing. Simplify everything.

CROSS-FUNCTIONAL TEAMS

There is a better way to work.

A way of working that improves the results we get on every project and with every initiative. This manner of working improves our communication, improves transparency, improves teamwork, and enables us to complete our work more quickly.

This model naturally results in improved culture and happier, more productive people.

Forming small cross-functional teams to perform our normal project and program work seems like a simple thing, but many IT organizations today continue to work in primarily silo-based teams. This is the traditional model and understandably is how many people continue to work today. If your organization has already moved beyond this model and you are working in cross-functional teams today, that is great news. You are likely seeing the benefits of working in this model. I've seen it firsthand many times. The benefits of working teams that represent two to four different functions across IT are exciting and very real.

When this shift has been made, there is no going back, and our people will recognize this change did not come to us soon enough.

Although the initial change to cross-functional teams will take some planning, a bit of effort, and won't be easy for some, once we make the transition to cross-functional teams in everything we do, the improvements will be clear to all the people participating in the new model, and the momentum and support for this improved structure will be clear. There is no going back.

For example, where the security organization would normally form a team to make progress on a new initiative, something like two-factor authentication on mobile devices, by forming a team of security experts, the new model of cross-functional teams would call us to include three or four other functional areas on the team to work side-by-side with the security team. For example, a representative from the PMO, the Service Desk, Governance, and the Datacenter would be a possible combination. Of course, your organization might be a bit different, but you get the idea. And you can use this simple example as a starting point.

The key is simple—to assemble strong thinkers who bring different experiences with different approaches and to turn them loose with the goal to craft a new and creative solution to a current business need.

This diverse set of skills and experiences will in virtually every case bring us a better result and a stronger solution. Our people are smart, very smart, and will recognize the benefits of working in cross-functional teams very quickly, and then it just becomes natural. It becomes how we always do things.

Cross-functional teams ask different questions and make better decisions as a result.

Another important point to make here is that we must take care to ensure these teams are recognized when a successful result is delivered. People thrive on recognition; we all love this simple but important validation of our efforts and hard work, so take the time to recognize members of the team when the project is completed, the deliverables done, and the initiative is a success. This both recognizes our people and at the same time supports, communicates, and validates the model of working in cross-functional teams. That singular act will draw people in and pull on our people to be part of this strategy in the future.

Even if your IT organization is not particularly great at team and individual recognition today, that is okay and very common. This is a great opportunity to use the deployment of these cross-functional teams as a fresh start and a new beginning to make celebrating success and recognition part of the culture. It is fun, it is easy, and the events can be small, casual, and inexpensive. The smallest and simplest recognition efforts pay back many times over and build a little more momentum in making cross-functional teams a success and in making our culture stronger and more passionate.

CHAPTER 3

PARTNERSHIP REDEFINED

Technology and Humanity working together is something to behold. Truly working together in a thoughtful and well-designed model that leverages the best of what each party has to offer.

This is not a token partnership that is smashed together quickly for convenience. That model would have limited value, would not evolve, and would not bring the lasting change we now have available to us.

A uniquely powerful force that is now possible framed in a new partnership for the first time in our thirty-year history of the IT organization—the opportunity for this new partnership has been created through the increased capabilities of intelligent technology and by a simultaneous increasing need for the unique skills of our people. Growing demands for increased investments in innovation and in building stronger customer relationships for example have created a stronger awareness of the value of our talented people. At the same time, AI, Robotics, and Automation technologies have advanced dramatically in the past ten years and in so doing have created the first opportunity to effectively delegate a significant block of the tactical/operational work that has burdened the people in IT for decades.

This is not intended to imply that this daily operational work is not important. It certainly is, and the IT organization and the business could not function without the performance of this foundational work. But we have an opportunity for the first time to delegate this work to technology and have it done quite well, in some cases even better than our people could perform the work. This assumes the work we will delegate fits the profile of well defined, structured, governed by clear business rules, relatively static, linear decision flow, and the other factors that make the task or business process a good candidate for automation and AI.

In this partnership model we delegate to technology the work it can perform better than humanity and focus humanity on what it is uniquely qualified to do and what technology is not capable of.

This remarkable combination is precisely what makes the new partnership model so intriguing.

We are effectively getting the best of both worlds—leveraging powerful technology to make everybody look better and work more effectively.

This partnership would not have been possible as recently as five years ago because technology was not up to the task.

But today, that has changed, and we can't ignore the accelerated evolution of AI, Robotics, and Automation. The advances of these technologies are compelling. And very good news for the IT organization is that the time has come to move many of our people into more strategic roles, which would not be possible if we didn't have the capability to step in and do a great job on the work that fits the aforementioned profile. It should be noted that this includes the high-volume and repetitive work that creates a challenge for the retention of our best people, who feel like they are being underutilized and are frustrated with the tactical nature of the job.

No problem, intelligent technology is happy and capable of stepping in and taking on this work and doing it to a very high standard.

One of the remarkable things about this new partnership is the degree to which each needs the other—intelligent technology desperately needs humanity to teach and share lest technology will be limited in its ability to grow and learn. At the same time, humanity needs technology to take on many of the operational and repetitive tasks that have blocked our people from taking on more strategic work and focusing, for the first time, on the more strategic work that needs our attention. And, there is another important consideration here that should not be overlooked, and that is the simple fact that many of the operational tasks can be performed better by technology. The right technology working on the right task or business process can likely complete the work faster, more consistently, and on demand versus the human model, who has limitations in all these areas.

This further calls attention to the power of this partnership—a combination that will enable humanity to be at its best, technology to be showcased like never before, and the real winners when this partnership achieves its potential are our customers and the business.

This is a very exciting future and well within our reach today.

THE BEST OF BOTH

The new partnership is not solely about making our people look their very best with little regard to what the role technology will occupy. Yes, this would be easy and convenient, but it would be limiting the long-term value of the Humanity|Technology partnership.

We must thoughtfully design the partnership in such a way that both humanity and technology can shine. In a way that both humanity and technology can grow and better support the other. This requires an objective look at the work that our people are best qualified to perform and, at the same time, an equally objective review of the work that intelligent technology is now able to perform. The details will depend on the given organization, the current staffing for the teams, and the technology that is available to deploy, but overall, we can consider the following guidelines:

Best Fits for Technology:

1. High-volume tasks
2. Highly repetitive work
3. Well-defined tasks and business processes
4. Work with well-understood business rules
5. Mature and unchanging business processes
6. After-hours services that can be automated
7. Work with structured and linear business processes
8. Work that is currently occupying the people we need on strategic initiatives
9. Work blocks that require a high speed of execution

10. Work processes that don't require active customer or user interaction

Best Fits for People:

1. Customer engagements
2. Work requiring active internal or external communications
3. Creative projects
4. Innovation initiatives
5. Business outreach programs
6. Programs focused on customer and user satisfaction
7. Immature and poorly defined business processes
8. Highly dynamic business processes
9. Mentoring programs
10. Customer retention programs
11. Partnership initiatives

This outline serves to provide your organization with a starting point for the discussions that should occur to evaluate and develop the plans that make sense for every unique combination of teams, people, experience, expertise, and technology portfolios. As such, this should be considered a baseline only and should be adapted to your requirements.

A key consideration that we need to emphasize here is that any plans require an evaluation of the people needed to staff the key strategic initiatives and then a review of the work these key people are currently assigned to. This then becomes a driver for our action plan; we simply can't be successful if we are unable to free these people, even if it is a portion of their time in the beginning, to shift these valuable skills over onto the strategic projects that will struggle or fail without the right people engaged.

Once we have identified the people required for the strategic projects, then assessed what work is currently occupying their time, we evaluate how we can offload as much of this work as possible onto the technology available in the IT portfolio, or plan to acquire the technology we need but that is not currently in-house. This might create a budget planning exercise and might take some time, but that is acceptable. Remember, we are building a framework for the next twenty-five years of the IT organization. It is worth the effort. Some steps in this process will take some time, and as such patience is important.

Figure 3.1 summarizes the process we have described above, and confirms the order in which these steps should be performed.

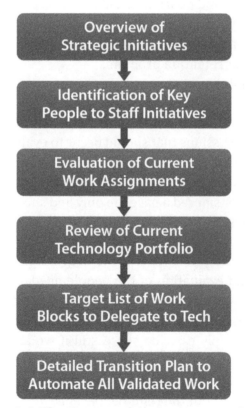

Figure 3.1 The Partnership Assessment Model

The sequence shown here is important, although the details of each step may vary from organization to organization.

Ultimately this is all about getting the right results and not about the process. The result we are seeking is the realignment of work across the IT organization that accomplishes the following simple goals:

A shift of our key people onto strategic projects

Leveraging technology to perform high-volume and repetitive work as a baseline

Extending technology to more complex and mid-level work by 2025–2030

90% Automation by the year 2025

An IT organization that operates effectively 24/7

With these goals met we will have ushered into reality the new partnership model. We will be leveraging the very best of technology with the very best of humanity, with the emphasis being on the latter, our talented people.

CLARITY OF PURPOSE

As so much change is happening today in the global marketplaces and in global cultures, the powerful forces of change are literally swirling around us as never before. The IT organization and the business can be searching for clarity, searching for purpose. This is fully understandable and should be recognized. With this challenge of change comes an opportunity for the new partnership model to bring us some of the much-needed strategy and purpose.

Yes, it is there if only we look.

The new partnership model between people and technology will enable us, in many cases for the first time, to make a meaningful shift of our talented people and our domain experts from the routine work of IT operations onto creative, innovation, and other strategic initiatives. This shift in itself is important. But there is far more value in play here: By shifting our people onto the high-impact, high-value initiatives, we are instantly creating a new level of focus and energy around these critical projects. No longer are our people disconnected from the strategy of IT and the core projects that drive the strategy. No longer are our people frustrated in that they are blocked from the most exciting work. They are now the beneficiaries of the shift, the new partnership, and are now in a position to have the greatest possible impact on the IT organization and on the full business. We can't underestimate the impact this change will have on our people. The leadership of IT is sending a clear signal that we are investing in our people and moving them into roles where they can have the biggest impact.

This reallocation of time for our people will bring a new sense of focus and a new sense of passion and excitement. And, of course, a new clarity of purpose.

This sense of purpose will better align the people staffing these initiatives with the strategy of IT and with the goals of the business. Our people will now have time to think about how each person, each team, and the organization can advance the strategy of IT. It is certainly not the case that our people lacked a commitment to the goals of IT in the past. The challenge has not been in the caring or in the commitment; the challenge has been in the daily demands on our people. And in many cases these demands have been dominated by tactical and operational work that makes up the majority of the escalations, tasks, and business processes that occur in IT every day. Even where there is a strong interest in advancing the strategy of IT and the strategic projects connected to this strategy, when our people are unable to be part of the effort, it creates a gap that can be discouraging. Our people hear about the strategy and goals of IT, and they may very well hear about new, exciting projects that are launching, but if the individual is not part of this effort, it is only natural there is disappointment about not being on the forefront of this exciting work.

The good news is that we can now change this model and pull many of these people into the effort. With an assist from technology as we build a plan to automate the very work that is blocking some of our best and brightest from joining the strategic initiatives, we now have the very real opportunity to make the shift and move our people onto the priority projects to ensure they are fully staffed with the right people. Never underestimate the excitement this will create, the energy that will be generated, and the sense of purpose each team will share.

By working on new creative projects, customer engagements, innovation teams, or business outreach programs, we are showing our people that they are the future, they are entrusted with meeting the critical challenges impacting the organization, and the leadership of the business is making an investment in them—reinforcing that our people are our greatest and most valuable asset. We are now putting them in a position to make a difference and make the most of their talents and experience every day.

Seems like good common sense perhaps, but in many cases this alignment of our people was not possible for many reasons. Today, that is changing and with some thoughtful planning and execution in support of the new Technology|Humanity partnership, we can free our people and enable technology to really shine.

With this helping hand from technology, our people can be at their very best. By tapping the unique creative and problem-solving skills of our people, we can put them in a position to really shine as well. And that brings us back to the value of this new partnership.

These benefits of assigning our key people to strategic projects and initiatives are only the beginning. We gain the additional upside in that our people will be happier, more motivated, more committed to the organization, more likely to remain with IT for a longer-term career, and much more. Recall that the very best IT organizations have the most tenured staff with ten-plus years being the benchmark, and the weakest IT organizations normally have a high turnover rate and an average tenure of two to three years. By keeping our people in place longer, we are benefiting the employee, the business, and the overall organization. All of this and we are achieving superior results with automation, with our innovation and customer-facing projects, and nurturing a happier and more productive set of teams across all of IT.

How good is that?

PEOPLE ELEVATED

Let's explore this idea of lifting up our people a bit more.

The partnership model between intelligent technology and our people is not simply about a partnership. Focusing on the partnership itself is important, but there is a much more important dimension to this partnership—and that is the enablement of our people to be transformed through the work that they perform every day. This is the lifting up of our people and making full use of their unique and priceless skills and experience.

The new partnership model is all about elevating the role of our people in the organization and enabling them to focus on the work that will determine the future success of the organization, the future stature of the business in your respective market. This is all about a strategic reallocation of the work that is performed across the IT organization today and for the first time viewing this work and bifurcating every task and business process into a work group that is fit for technology and a work group that is fit for our people. This separation and delegation were not possible before; we did not have adequately capable and adaptable technology ready to receive a meaningful segment of the work and to then be successful in executing this important work group every day. The need was there of course to free our people from the operational and tactical work that occupies so much of their time, but a capable partner did not yet exist.

Today, that has changed.

Intelligent technology has taken a quantum leap forward over the past ten years, and what was not possible only a decade ago is now routine for the new generation of technology. With this advancement, we can now increase our focus on people and begin this very thoughtful and deliberate shift of how our people spend their time.

To put this in perspective, approximately 50-75% of the time our people spend on current activities today will shift to new strategic projects over the next five years. This will result in a few important benefits:

Reaching the goal of a 90% automated IT organization by the year 2025

A dramatic increase in the amount of work performed on strategic initiatives

Superior execution of high-volume and repetitive tasks

The IT organization offering all services 24/7

A happier, more motivated, and longer tenured IT staff

From these few examples you will begin to see the dramatic impact of the new Technology|Humanity partnership and resulting new focus of our people.

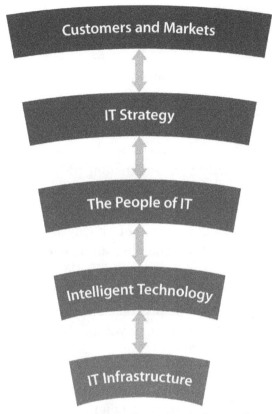

Figure 3.2 The Elevation of People

The headline for all of this should be about leveraging the talents of our people and placing them in positions to leverage their unique abilities and to really shine. But let's give credit where credit is due, and that is with technology. Note that two to three of our example benefits above are made possible by the capabilities of the new generation of technology. We should further note than the work won't simply be performed by technology; it will in fact be performed better than it was before. This improvement is in taking advantage of new intelligent technology that is able to perform at a remarkable rate of speed, able to perform structured tasks with 100% consistency, able to scale with no limits in most cases, and able to perform 24/7 into an unlimited horizon. These simple four examples are remarkable in what they represent in terms of the contribution of technology to the partnership—both taking on important segments of work, but at the same time performing that work to a new and higher standard.

This once again reminds us of the important contribution technology will make in the future of the IT organization.

Taking this a step further, the outstanding performance of technology in these areas further enables us to elevate the roles of our people and increase their focus on the work and initiatives that have been lacking the attention of our highly skilled people for decades. And at the same time, enabling our people to be fully focused on these strategic projects, knowing technology has the other stuff under control and is doing it very well. This is vital, in that we won't be pulling our people off their projects constantly to run back to the operational work. Technology will be doing the work exceptionally well.

Once again, this brings us back to our people being elevated as only they can be and now fully engaged where they can make the most difference—happy, productive, and excited about building a new future for the IT organization.

It's a truly remarkable model and not an exaggeration to call this the beginning of a new era for the IT organization and the business.

TECHNOLOGY WITH A PURPOSE

As it is important to ensure our people have a purpose, it is equally important to ensure we take the time to define and communicate the purpose of technology. This purpose is not solely a human thing. It is important that both parties of the new partnership understand with absolute clarity what work and role(s) each is responsible for and how each will be successful.

In the traditional IT model, technology was typically deployed in a reactive manner, where it was immediately necessary or convenient. This model required a minimum amount of thought and planning because the abilities of technology were limited and focused on specific areas. Technology was considered to be simply a tool, much like a hammer, capable of performing a specific task in order to create a specific outcome. Today, a new generation of intelligent technology can accommodate a much broader and more advanced range of work, and these abilities are advancing every day.

For example, a Chat Bot at the time of this writing is capable of handling—and handling very effectively—a live chat session with an employee or customer. The Bot can always be available and can quickly and effectively answer common questions and perform a series of defined tasks. This is not intended to imply the Bot is simplistic; the Bot is in fact very capable, and customer satisfaction has proven to be high with most Bot sessions. With this example, we place technology in a well-defined role and with a purpose that enables the technology to be successful and provide an important service. Further, the Bot enables the people currently filling these roles to move into one of the innovation, customer relationship, business outreach, communications, or creative roles we have discussed repeatedly.

This is a fantastic example of technology with a purpose, then enabling people with a purpose, and both our wonderful people and the advanced technology performing in roles that enable them to be successful. And by being successful we have then likely improved the performance of each of the respective functions and improved the overall performance of the organization at the same time.

> *Technology with a purpose, and with for-purpose ability and strong performance.*

> *People with a purpose, and with for-purpose ability and outstanding performance.*

This is a great snapshot of the very real partnership that is available to us today, and for the first time. We have used the example of the Chat Bot, but it could have been many other examples, and this availability of many examples is in itself a good thing. We have never had such a rich portfolio of intelligent technology from which to choose and from which to draw on to further extend the partnership.

It's important to remember that we don't arrive at the right model by accident. This requires careful planning and evaluating the jobs to be done and the technology we have available to fill those roles. The need for planning is now more important than ever because we have such a rich set of technology available to help—this is a very good problem to have, if we can call it a problem for the sake of this discussion.

It helps to create an inventory of all the tasks and business processes that are candidates for automation, and to then create a similar inventory of all the technology we have available in the IT portfolio to fill the automation needs.

This is the first step, matching up the candidates for automation with the technology we have to step into that role.

This first phase will identify our initial fits and will in itself bring a great deal of value. There will be some number of clear matches that enable us to automate a set of tasks and business processes, and in each case we will have individuals or teams who are then free to be redirected to other work on our strategic initiatives list of priorities. Take this process step by step, and start with this first step in order to make the best use of what is available today.

The second phase will then be to identify additional tasks, business processes, or roles that are a good candidate for automation, but for which we currently don't have the right technology in the IT portfolio. This would then represent a strategic investment that can bring additional automation to the organization, thereby meeting the other goals we have discussed around speed of performance, consistent execution, and 24/7 operations. But, even more importantly, we get the dual benefit of once again freeing our people who are currently being occupied by the work that will be automated.

This further catapults the IT organization into a new model. It's a case of advancing two strategic agendas simultaneously, something that has been rare in the history of IT but is now available to us and fully under our control.

We will close this discussion with a reminder to be disciplined and methodical with this approach as follows:

> *Identify the tasks, business processes, and roles that are candidates for automation.*
>
> *Create an inventory of the technologies that are available to fill these needs.*

Assess the fit-for-purpose score for each technology.

Evaluate the people and time that will be freed from a successful automation.

Identify the strategic work we can then shift these same people to.

Of course, it is always a good idea to put your own unique requirements and circumstances into this model and make it your own, but the structure and rigor are important to ensure we get a good result.

This realignment of the work, of technology, and of our people will be a top priority for all IT organizations over the next decade. When performed well, it's no exaggeration to observe that it will fundamentally change how work is performed every day, and how the IT organization will serve employees and customers in a superior manner.

CHAPTER 4

MENTAL HEALTH

The fundamental need to better serve and nurture our people must bring with it an increased awareness on mental health.

The IT organization today faces higher expectations, more pressure to deliver to the business, and continued budget constraints, a shortage of qualified workers, a further acceleration of technology, increased security threats, and much more. All of this creates an increasingly stressful and demanding workplace for the people of IT, and this pace of advancement and the escalating expectations are unlikely to abate any time soon.

This stress is taking a toll on our people—a significant toll that must be acknowledged and managed, because it has much to do with the future health of the IT organization and of the business.

The challenge we face is made only more critical in that this issue of mental health and well-being has rarely been addressed in the history of IT. This is not to imply we did not consider the health of our people important, for that has certainly not been the case.

It has more been a matter of mental health not being visible to us every day, something that we can't see and therefore something we don't have a clear reminder of in the course of our work every day. But make no mistake, the struggles of our people are very real and connected to the future success of the IT organization.

In this chapter we will take a closer look at this critical issue. In some cases our discussion will take a familiar course and may recommend actions your organization has already put into place. In other cases we will explore considerations around mental health that will be new and unconventional, with a goal for all of us to see this challenge differently and with a new degree of urgency. We can't underestimate the toll multiple priorities, stress, pressure to deliver against aggressive schedules, balancing the workplace with our personal lives, a more demanding customer, and other mounting expectations take on our people every day.

The challenge of mental health is complex and continues to evolve given the remarkable evolution of the global marketplace and the changing demands of our culture. But it is complex, and it is not possible to address all the considerations of mental health in this discussion, so our goal for this chapter is to increase awareness first and foremost, and to then propose a few basic strategies to help address and manage the many demands created through mental health challenges.

There is no single solution, so it's important we work together across the IT organization and the business to grow awareness and to do our part to address this growing risk. This is not simply a management issue—every member of the IT organization shares some responsibility for improving the mental health of all of our people. This must become a cultural priority and a focus for all of us in working together to improve our own mental health as well as the mental health of our teammates in IT and the people we work with across the business.

It is an inescapable truth that a happy and healthy workforce is a more productive and a more successful workforce.

This emphasis on healthy extends to both physical health and mental health; these two things are closely linked. Our focus here is on mental health because it is in need of more attention in the modern, digital, and mobile workplace, but that should not reduce our awareness and commitment to the partner of physical health.

As with many other topics we address throughout the book, the guidelines we will discuss on mental health seem like good common sense, and they certainly are. But despite what might appear to be crystal clear to us upon reflection, the challenge of mental health has often not been a clear priority for the IT organization. It has not been natural to us as a culture so focused on technology and our many systems and tools that require so much of our time and energy.

Fortunately, that is changing today, and we are more committed than ever before to our people, to our teams, and to building a new culture for the future of IT.

A NEW PRIORITY

The beginning to a real improvement in mental health across the culture of the IT organization is a simple one—making mental health a priority, making it a core point of emphasis in building our new culture.

We will find that once we have established this priority and communicated our support for this focus, we will immediately see strong support and many willing partners.

Managers today are better equipped than ever to support their team members in working together toward improving mental health. Every employee across all IT teams understand this is an important and serious issue and one that needs our attention. The Human Resources organization is ready and willing to partner with IT in advancing our focus and creating a structure to ensure we maintain the appropriate level of priority around mental health and don't lose our way.

All of this energy and capability is there for us and only in need of a push, a focus, and a commitment to bring our efforts to bear on the issue. It only takes a little encouragement. Our people fundamentally know this will help all of us, and we are ready to do our part.

It is truly amazing what our people can do when we give them a chance and then let them go to work. I can think of no more important priority over the next decade than to ensure we are nurturing a healthy and productive workplace full of passion and energy.

This is an unstoppable force of good.

The shift in culture begins when we call out mental health as a critical issue for the IT organization and one we will focus on and invest in for the foreseeable future.

This change is as simple as a communication from IT leadership and then the subsequent follow-up throughout our teams and in the many discussions every manager will have with their teams and direct reports. This should happen every day and become part of the normal dialogue we have in IT. As the commitment to mental health is established, some simple training can make a big difference. This training will serve to arm all our people with the right level of understanding and some basic guidelines for what we can all watch for in our coworkers that represents an employee in need of our support and possible further specialized assistance. Which brings us back to fundamental mental health awareness—the beginning of changing our culture and thereby enlisting every person in the IT organization to be part of the extended team that identifies people in need of help.

Over time, we all have setbacks and we all have bad days. But for some, the feeling of discouragement and frustration can be more serious and can feel overwhelming. It is at this critical time that each of us can recognize a coworker who is hurting and can use a little help, a bit of encouragement, or in some cases more extensive attention. It is important that we all work together to catch this early and potentially prevent some normal and expected discouragement from growing into something more serious.

A strong and healthy IT culture creates a sense of community and caring that elevates our awareness of many things that can challenge our people and our organization. This happens in every organization everywhere and is absolutely human. It is then those businesses with a strong culture and a commitment to improving mental health are equipped to identify and act quickly and smartly when any one of us is struggling and needs a helping hand. When the needed help is provided to a member of IT, it is a remarkable thing and noticed immediately by others; it sends a clear signal of caring that every person will appreciate because we all know that time might come when we are the one who needs help and the people all around us will be ready.

This growing circle of support, attention, and preparation all begins with the simple act of communicating mental health as a priority and making some time—a little time makes a big difference—to ensure we keep mental health on the list of priorities, we have time dedicated to this topic in staff meetings, and the organization is providing training and ongoing education forums for mental health into the future. Remember, the Human Resources team will be a great partner in assisting IT on this initiative and can assist the IT organization in building a more complete plan to address mental health than we could on our own.

Beyond the HR team, there are many other resources in the marketplace that can help with mental health awareness, readiness plans, training, and much more. This critical issue is worthy of our time and resources.

STRESS IS EVERYWHERE

As the world continues to change around us, the demands on finding a balance between our work and personal lives becomes more complicated, our always-on culture demands more of our time around the clock, expectations continue to rise for the IT organization, and many more factors are colliding to elevate the stress we feel every day. This stress is difficult to manage for even the most experienced of our staff and even more so for our talented workers who have less experience.

The growth of stress is a direct contributor to the challenges of mental health, and stress is also directly linked to our physical health in addition to the toll it takes on mental well-being. The overall wellness of every worker in the IT organization and across the business is closely connected to our ability or inability to manage stress.

To start, the responsibility of managing stress falls to each one of us. Although many of us share common challenges and similar circumstances, we are all unique, and there is no single formula for how stress is created and how we can effectively manage all it brings. It is a matter of good common sense and finding an approach that works for managing the many vectors of stress and keeping the risk stress creates in our lives at a manageable level. It is simply not possible to completely eliminate stress—it comes along with any job, and higher levels of stress are common for many of the roles across the IT organization. As trusted stewards of the technology and data of the business, valuable and strategic assets for sure, the stress that accompanies many jobs in the

IT organization today is exceptionally high and likely to continue growing into the future.

Job Demands   Financial
Relationships   Parenting
Hardships   Economy

— Stress —

Uncertainty   Health
New Job   Family Care
Budgets   School

Figure 4.1 The Vectors of Stress

In many ways the stress that comes with the IT organization is simply part of the fabric of the modern business given the responsibility associated with security threats, delivering great service, managing vast amounts of corporate data, as well as ensuring the IT infrastructure is healthy and available—and this is just the beginning. Each of these elements reflects the importance of the technology and data in driving the strategy and operations of the modern business and reminds us once again that a business can't find success in today's global marketplace in the absence of alignment between technology and the broader business.

Recognizing that the IT organization is now inextricably linked to the future success of every small, medium, and enterprise business brings us a heightened sense of responsibility, and where there is great responsibility, there is sure to be great stress. We can't ignore this mounting pressure and must work together as teammates and as the full IT organization to manage the challenges this all creates.

Because stress can't be completely eliminated from the workplace, it helps to have some practical strategies for keeping stress in check, and in protecting our precious physical and mental health.

A few simple things to remember:

Recognize the warning signs of stress and how it affects you.

Develop a few activities and outlets that help combat stress.

Actively pursue your passions outside the workplace.

Watch for signs of stress in coworkers and offer to help.

Discuss any stress challenges with your manager.

Find a few charitable activities that enable you to help others.

Be honest with yourself when stress begins to grow.

A day away from work at the right time can work wonders.

Pay attention to your nutrition—eating healthy is a great way to combat stress.

Exercise regularly—even walking for thirty minutes a few times a week really helps.

It is likely you are aware of and have implemented some things on this list, but perhaps there are a few more you can take on going forward.

Managing stress is a case of a few small things making a big difference. There is no secret, no magic formula for combatting stress, and we are all different, so what works for a friend or a coworker might not work for you.

The key is in being aware that stress can be a serious threat to our mental and physical well-being. It is a constant presence in our workplace and culture today, and each of us needs to find a simple formula that works in helping us to manage risk and keep it at acceptable levels.

We are in this together for the long run, and we won't be able to remake the wonderful world of IT quickly, so it requires us to be at our best every day, day after day. We simply can't accept stress slowing us down and blocking us from the exciting future of IT.

AWARENESS AND SUPPORT

Mental health is vital to our future in the workplace and in our personal lives outside our jobs, and we have so much opportunity each day to support, encourage, and celebrate with one another. This is very much a team- and community-driven effort that brings us a new sense of awareness and the constant need to support the people who surround us every day.

When faced with a challenge, in particular large and serious challenges, there is also opportunity right there in front of us. And it helps our energy and our resolve to focus on the opportunity and not allow the challenge to overwhelm us.

In this case, the opportunity is to elevate awareness of mental health challenges for now and for the future. This is a new lifestyle in the workplace and for the IT organization. The demands of the global, always-on economy and the growing and relentless demands and pressures of business will create a constant set of demands on the dedicated workers of the IT organization for today and into the future. We are all in this together. I have never encountered a member of IT staff who was not fully dedicated to helping teammates and the broader IT organization better manage the demands of the workplace. We can make the case that the dependency the modern business has on technology and on data today creates an even larger set of expectations on the IT organization and a closer linkage between the IT staff and every member of the broader organization. Think about the critical role that technology—and the vast amounts of data and the important learning it holds—has on the daily performance of the organization and of the ultimate success of the business.

We raise this point yet again to help us appreciate the opportunity we collectively have as the IT organization to support and lead the business into the future, while at the same time understanding why the daily motion and expectations on the IT organization feel so significant today—more demanding than ever and likely to continue to grow into the foreseeable future. This rising set of expectations on the IT organization is a natural part of the exciting future we see for the teams of IT. And this linkage is an important one to understand when we look at the need for awareness and support for every member of the IT organization for the future and for the vital role of mental health in the transformation of IT.

It would not be difficult to make a case for the IT organization as being the single most impacted by the challenges of mental health over the next twenty-five years. It is certainly true that mental health is prominent on the agenda for all of the business, but there are unique and accelerating pressures on the IT organization in particular. A few contributors to this growing pressure include:

The dramatic increase in security threats

Escalated demands of governance and compliance

The remarkable impact of intelligent technologies on business

The inherent accountability of managing corporate data

The growing risks associated with the explosion of mobile devices

The pressures of around-the-clock access to corporate infrastructure

A global shortage of skilled technology workers

Relentless global competition in every market segment

Each of these examples holds an important story and unique set of considerations and demands, and this is only the beginning.

It is hard to overstate how important it is when a person we work with, a friend, or a member of our family shows a desire to help us overcome one of the many large or small challenges that inevitably come our way. Think back to a time when you were in need of help and somebody was there to help lift you up.

Remember how that made you feel. Remember that incredible sense of gratitude you felt. Remember how it likely made the difference between your moving forward or becoming mired in feelings of hopelessness or discouragement. It is a fine line, and often the difference is another person offering a little help.

A brief word of encouragement, a little positive feedback, it can be anything that makes a big difference. This helping hand is the front line for our important work in committing to helping and supporting our teammates in overcoming the challenges that lie ahead and thereby enable us to experience success together when we seize the remarkable opportunities that lie before us in the future of the new IT organization.

LIFE BALANCE

So much of our future together will be about balance—the precious balance of all that demands our time—and in finding the right balance, we will with few exceptions find happiness and health, both mental and physical. Physical and mental health go together, although the focus here is on mental health because it is so often neglected in business and certainly in the IT organization. It is a good start to begin with mental health and then on the journey to better mental well-being, we can add adjustments that will improve our physical health.

It is a simple relationship. When we are happy, we are likely to experience improved mental health. And taking this one step further, when we improve our physical health, we are likely to feel better and to be happier, and this then carries over into the precious improvement of our mental health.

It is a good strategy to ask oneself a few simple questions:

What makes you happy?

What is missing in your life today?

Is there something in your daily life that brings you great joy?

Similarly, is there something in your daily life that brings sadness?

When you are at your happiest, what created that feeling?

I'm certainly no mental health professional and have no professional training on mental health, so I can only offer a few common-sense guidelines based on forty years of business experience and some successes tempered with plenty of failures; enough to have an opinion.

And my humble opinion begins with this—mental health is really important, more important than ever both today and over the next decade, and mental health becomes all but unattainable without finding some sense of life balance.

It is too often true that many of us as dedicated professionals are willing to do "whatever it takes" to ensure success in our business and in the workplace, beginning the formulation of life balance with the work side and then determining what is left over for our personal lives. Sometimes there is plenty left over and sometimes there is very little left over. Normally, the latter.

I'm proposing a different approach—let's turn this traditional model upside down and begin with our home/family/personal lives and determine what makes us truly happy,

what makes us fulfilled outside the workplace, calibrate our life balance to this side, and then determine what we have left to give to our professional role.

Now, of course we need to be responsible, and I'm not suggesting that we spend the high majority of our day fishing or riding bikes or really elevating our cooking game in the kitchen. We do after all have a fundamental need to provide for our families, and the simple economics of life can't be ignored.

Long-term unemployment is not a good strategy for most of us, my friends.

What I am suggesting is that we devote a new level of attention to our personal needs, which become a new baseline, and then we build our professional commitments around this new baseline. Of course, for the entirety of modern business, most of us have permitted our professional responsibilities to dominate the division of our time. For many people with demanding positions, the needs of our jobs have grown to the point where we have very little left for our family, our friends, our significant others, and our personal passions. Then these job demands have only grown and expanded over the years and decades.

Taking a step back, this is a reckoning that is long overdue and most of us would agree with the need to reevaluate how our time every day is invested. Time is so precious. There are certainly practical considerations, and providing the basics of food and shelter are a constant that can't be ignored. But once we have completed this new and fresh view of where we wish to spend our time every day and how we can enrich our lives outside the workplace and enjoy the journey of life more than ever before, it is often possible to find creative ways to complete our work more quickly and effectively and thereby create the priceless time we need to rebalance our lives.

If we wait for the opportunity to reallocate this time to come, if we hope there will be the perfect time to recalibrate our days, and that is somewhere ahead of us, that time will never come, and the perfect opportunity will never materialize. So we need to take a step back and take a fresh view of our life balance now. This fresh look is a key to mental health and to our long-term well-being in the workplace and therefore critical to our ultimate happiness and sense of fulfillment.

Having watched some people close to me go through this process and having been through this process myself, I can attest that it is a remarkable experience. In some cases, it could result in your staying in your current job and making a few needed adjustments to find a better life balance as a result. In other cases, you might find that a natural career change or a new role has been in your heart for some time, and it is now time to make that shift. And in other cases still, it could result in a dramatic shift in the path you are traveling, now taking a leap of faith and accepting some risk that could lead to an exciting and fulfilling future that might have seemed impossibly out of reach in the past.

Only you can find what is right, and I can only offer encouragement to not wait. Now is the time to take the small steps or the big leap into a new future—one that will bring you a wholly new sense of excitement and fulfillment.

We can accomplish anything and we can be anything if only we make the decision that now is the time, and we are willing to take a chance on ourselves and remake our future.

You can do it.

CHAPTER 5

THE WORKDAY EVOLVED

The workday is changing like never before, right before our eyes and at a dizzying pace. The workday is an embodiment of so much we have discussed throughout the book, including mental health, cultural change, the partnership with technology, a new workforce, and much, much more. In many ways, the workday itself represents a collision of all these factors and is a reflection of the future of the IT organization.

We simply can't keep doing things the same way. We have to work smarter, more efficiently, more focused, and with a greater sense of our priorities. All of the implied strategy here and our view of how business will function in the future will be captured and advanced, or stunted, by the workday.

Starting with the basics, the workday must be more flexible and more in line with our new imperatives while at the same time creating the opportunity for us to be more productive in a given block of time. It would be naïve to believe that we can somehow overnight turn our collective backs on the responsibilities and deliverables that make up the daily work of the IT organization. If anything, these demands have grown and will continue to grow. This is the reality of the IT organization today—we are feeling increased pressure from the global marketplace, from demanding customers, and from across the business.

Yet, at the same time we are experiencing a crisis of stress, mental health, life balance, quality of life, and much more. So, we find ourselves faced with the need to find a new and more effective way to work, a new lifestyle, if you will, that addresses the needs on both sides of this essential equation. A workday that enables us to complete the necessary work, in many cases better than before, while enabling us to complete the realignment and rebalancing of our life priorities as we discussed in Chapter 4 and throughout the book. The relentless pursuit of happiness, fulfillment, and enjoying our personal journey like never before.

This then gives us a fun topic to take on in this chapter and elsewhere, and we will explore some simple and new approaches to this challenge of the workday.

The simple fact is that for most adults, the beginning of every Monday through Friday represents the start of a workday in some form. This is a timeless cultural rhythm and one practiced by our parents and their parents before them for many generations.

Going to work every day was just what we did and how we lived.

Now that has changed like never before.

The new model recognizes a new and necessary balance between our personal needs and our professional needs. We take those on each day in balance, and in many cases we begin with the needs outside our job, what must be done today, how we can accomplish that list, and then with what remains how we can successfully complete what our job requires.

This balance assumes a number of factors that are increasingly true, with a few examples being:

More people are willing to work outside traditional hours.

Mobile devices and smartphones provide a new level of work flexibility.

It is less necessary to be physically in an office to accomplish our work.

New technologies enable us to work more quickly and from anywhere.

The workday might now consist of mixed segments of work and play.

Weekdays and weekends are now changing, and we aren't following the traditional model—these days now look more alike.

Most of us will agree with these examples, and they bring us back to the ability to simply accomplish our personal goals each day, complete our work more effectively and more quickly, and ultimately to be happier.

We are able to accomplish our personal goals, our checklist, each day and to be very productive in our job and all at the same time. This might require us to take an early morning or evening conference call, or to answer a few emails on Saturday, or to review a short document while attending an event for one of our kids, but these are increasingly acceptable tradeoffs in order to bring us more flexibility and more freedom throughout the average workday.

A final comment on the workday—the writing of this book is overlapping with the global pandemic of 2020, and I am struck that the reality of the quarantine and home-based work and school for most people and families around the world will further accelerate the evolution of the workday. The quarantine and the virtual elimination of any in-office work and business travel have caused us to rethink much of what we do every day and how we work.

This dramatic shift created by COVID-19 in our daily schedule has created a new path but, I would propose, only accelerated the evolution of the workday that was already naturally occurring and likely to bring us to the same place and the same workday model only ten to fifteen years sooner.

MORE WITH LESS

This is a wonderfully powerful and simple idea we begin with as we contemplate the evolution of the workday. Achieving more with less is a powerful idea and strategy that will guide the future of how we work and how we live. Creating more output, completing more deliverables and more success with less time and effort is a goal that all of us can agree to. But this attractive goal quickly becomes a question of "how?" Is it even possible? Is it within reach for me? Is it a key to happiness? Is it a practical path that can lead to future professional success?

I believe the answer to all these questions is a sound "yes." The key to making the strategy of *more with less* a reality is a matter of some fundamental planning and a commitment to work within the guidelines of our plan every day. Most of us would agree that seems reasonable, so then what does that look like?

There is no single right place to start this discussion, so we will begin with a few guidelines that will assist our planning and actions for making *more with less* a reality and thereby changing the average workday. To get us started, consider the following:

> *Identify the top five priorities in your current role. Validating these top five priorities will determine all, or the majority of, your success.*

> *Identify all work that does not support these top five priorities (often 50% or more).*

Create a plan to delegate or eliminate the nonessential 50%+ of the work. The goal should be to eliminate the work altogether.

Identify one strategic initiative you are not actively working currently.

Allocate approximately 10% of your time to this strategic initiative.

Create a simple process of checkpoints to validate the plan is working. Weekly checkups are a good baseline to catch any issues early.

Carefully guard against slipping back into old habits.

Continue checkpoints to ensure your time allocation is in the top priorities.

Write a list of personal questions and statements to hold yourself accountable.

Some of this is good common sense, but what we must create is a new alignment of our precious time to the top priorities of our job and to then be more focused and more productive every day.

This focus and productivity are not attainable without a good idea of priorities and the work that can create the biggest impact on the organization.

From this it further follows that it is not possible to ignore the key elements of success in our jobs. What is far too common is to have nonessential work demanding large blocks of our time and reducing our ability to accomplish the most important tasks. This reflects a natural accumulation of work over time, and it slowly builds, for many reasons, until it reaches the point where we are spending the majority of our time on the work that will ultimately not determine our personal success or the success of our business. This is more common than we would like to believe or recognize, and a source of frustration and lower productivity than we desire to have.

So, the time has come for a realignment of how we invest our time—long overdue in many cases—and we can't afford to wait. Now is the time. The essence of this is very simple—focus on what is most important, take a step forward with the time we have allocated to strategic work, and eliminate the tactical and lower-value work that is demanding so much of our time. This tactical work is a trap and one that blocks us from a happier and more productive future. This shift begins with a vetting process that makes a lot of sense for many reasons. It is a key to truly achieving more with less and making a meaningful change in our average workday, creating a new beginning for what each day looks like.

Sound like a crazy dream? It's not. It's within our reach.

Most members of the IT organization are frustrated with how their time is allocated every day. Although this is common in business today and certainly not unique to IT, we can make a case that the good people of IT have unique challenges due to the sheer growth in the volume of work placed on the IT organization as a natural byproduct of the growth of technology and the role it holds in the day-to-day operation of every business. Technology is now central to how we conduct our work and execute the business processes that make up the fabric of the modern business.

The longer we wait the more difficult it becomes to make this shift—to create a new model for how we think and how we work every day. In the beginning it is not easy to overcome old habits and change old instincts, what is really a form of addiction to the operational and tactical work that can demand our time and attention every day. Yes, it can be satisfying to check things off our list and complete work that is right there in front of us, easy to define and easy to see. It does bring a level of satisfaction and some sense of productivity.

But this is a trap. This is a bad habit of sorts.

This is the very work that will never change the future of the business, brings little real value, and is quite effective at blocking us from the strategic and high-impact work that can change the future of the business and the course of our careers.

This shift is truly a lifestyle change. We are reprogramming how we see each day and the work that each day is composed of.

I do understand that making this change and creating a new lifestyle is not easy, it is not natural, because we must overcome how we have worked for most of our careers. But this is a case of disruption, a case where we must disrupt ourselves before our job or our organization is lost or taken from us. This might seem extreme, but this is exactly what will happen. It is only a matter of time.

CONVENIENCE AND SPEED

As we undertake to make this lasting change in lifestyle, we begin to appreciate like never before the importance of convenience and speed—two wonderfully simple and powerful ideals—and as we will see, these two principles naturally complement one another.

Convenience improves our quality of life, saves us time, makes us more productive, and makes us happy. Perhaps the most important of all is that last point, happiness. Who doesn't like convenience? We are naturally drawn to all things that are easy and save us time. This is not just the providence of our personal lives but now an important consideration in our work lives as well.

A few examples of convenience that directly impact our professional productivity and ones that I've experienced in recent years:

Smartphone access to company email

Smartphone access to calendars and meeting information

Managing expense reports on mobile devices

Conference calling and video calling on mobile devices

Each of these activities are game-changers, and although we now tend to take them for granted, the initial introduction of these technologies and apps over the past ten years made a huge impact on how we manage our time. These examples and others now enable us to be productive in performing our jobs at any time and from anywhere. This is simply stated, but what it really means is extraordinary. For so many years our ability to perform our jobs was connected to a physical corporate office and the planning of our schedules this implies—an office where we were required to be for a meeting, to participate on a conference call, to complete and distribute reports, to make photocopies, to access corporate applications, including email and HR systems, and much, much more. Yes, this was how we worked every day. So much time was invested and potentially wasted in placing ourselves in the right location at the right time to ensure we can do our jobs.

Now, we expect more and have less tolerance for the traditional model that connects us to an office or a building.

And there is no going back.

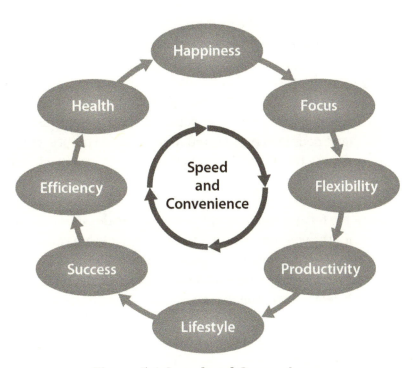

Figure 5.1 Speed and Convenience

A key distinction to make in this discussion is the driver for this model of convenience and speed. We seek this combination because it enables us to be more productive in our jobs in order to create more time to pursue what is really central to our future, our overall happiness, beginning with what makes us happy in our personal lives. More time to invest in our families, more time for our passions and in all pursuits that will ultimately bring us fulfillment, contentment, and overall health. For too long we have compromised in our lives outside work in order to pursue success in our careers. With convenience and speed, we can now be more productive in our jobs—in fact do great work in our jobs, perhaps better than ever, with less waste and less time invested—in order to create the flexibility and time we need to invest in happiness outside our jobs. To give more of ourselves to those things that have been limited and under pressure due to the many demands of our jobs.

Don't think for a moment this might compromise the success of the IT organization or of the role we perform.

The very opposite is true. This rebalancing of our time, our workday, and everything related to daily performance of our job will make for more productive, fully satisfied, fully committed, and more engaged people across IT and a more powerful presence of Humanity for the future of IT. This builds a better and stronger future for all of us.

Our use of the term *convenience* here is not a reckless shortcut; it is at its essence the very opposite. A <u>truly convenient thing</u> enables us to accomplish an equivalent or superior result with less time and effort expended. This is a powerful idea, approaching magic in the capability it represents. Due to advances in technologies and infrastructure, the opportunity to pursue true convenience—a convenience upgrade, you might say—in every phase of our lives is now more possible than ever.

Good questions to ask ourselves from time to time are:

How can I make this task more convenient?

How can this work be easier to complete?

How can I make this work more enjoyable to perform?

Is there any part of this work that does not make sense?

How can I achieve the same result in less time?

How can I achieve more with the same amount of time and effort?

These questions are simple examples to give you an idea of how we want to approach the goals of convenience and speed. You should, of course, add your own questions to what can be a self-inspection tool—a useful checkpoint in everything we do.

We should never stop searching for ways to save time and to accomplish more with the same amount of effort and time, or better yet to accomplish an equal result with less time and effort. Seems like just good common sense. But in many cases we have not committed to asking these questions and searching for a better way.

This curiosity becomes a habit, a lifestyle, and when we commit to asking the questions and searching for answers, we are likely to find them. We are likely to find a better way. We are likely to save time and accomplish more with less.

THE BALANCE OF WORK AND HOME

The workday is a constant in the lives of most, the fundamental need to have a job in order to provide for our basic needs and, for some people, the needs of a family. With this idea of the workday being a given, we must find a new balance that enables us to meet the goals of our role in the workplace, while at the same time elevating our focus on our personal lives and meeting our goals of happiness and mental health. Most of this statement is nothing new and would be true for our parents and our grandparents before them—many generations of workers have faced the challenge of balancing the demands of work and home.

What has changed is our approach to finding this balance. With new economic conditions, new technologies to help us live our lives differently, the reality of increased job stress, and the challenges of mental health in the IT organization, we now take a new and different view of this challenge of *balance*. A complex issue for sure, and one that is very personal to each of us. While it is true that no two people are exactly the same in what we seek in this balance, and our priorities can be very different and changing over time, there are a few fundamental principles that we can apply to the process of finding the balance. What follows are a few suggestions to help get the process started:

> *Know your top few priorities and goals for home life—a short list of three to five is a good model—and keep it simple.*
>
> *What is the one must-have for your life outside work?*

What is the biggest thing missing in your home life currently?

What is the top goal for your job this year?

What is the one key thing missing in your job currently?

How will success be defined in your job over the next two to three years?

Note the focus on priorities. This is necessary because we can't attempt to find a new balance without a clear definition of priorities. We can't accomplish everything, so what are the few key things that are critical at work and at home?

Take the time to think carefully about this. It helps to make a few notes, put them aside, and then come back to them a few times over the next few days or more if needed. Be honest with yourself and think through what you currently feel good about and what is missing or creating challenges at home or at work. This is an opportunity to make some changes and bring you closer to the happiness you want and deserve.

We should not wait. Now is the best time to make a few adjustments. Waiting won't make this easier, only harder in most cases. Waiting also takes a toll on the many people who currently are unhappy with a work and home balance that is tilted in favor of work. This forces workers to pay a tax that for some is understood and acceptable; for others it is a tax on our personal lives that can't be part of our future. There are certainly those people who today have the right balance with work and home, and that is fantastic. They no doubt have been proactive and thoughtful in making adjustments to priorities and how time is spent every day. This discussion won't offer anything new to these people who are already working in the model that other people are working toward. If you are fortunate enough to have a friend or colleague who has met this challenge of balance successfully, they are probably happy to discuss their own journey with you. When we can learn from a teammate or friend, we should.

Good advice is priceless. Take it when it is available and don't look back.

Just remember those times a mentor or friend helped you, and don't miss a chance to help others when the opportunity is there. Giving back is a remarkable and rewarding experience.

For those of us who continue to search for the right balance—with our notes on what is most important to us at home and at work, and the list of questions shown above—we can go through the exercise of making adjustments to the balance of work and home. What has worked for me personally and what has worked for others I have supported and coached is to keep this process simple. Focus on the very few important things that will make a difference in the quality of our lives. Attempting to make too many adjustments too quickly is likely to be a frustrating experience and will fail to have the impact we are seeking. Few means few, so look for the two or three things that mean the most and will tip the balance and enrich our lives outside of work in ways that can have a remarkable and lasting impact on our happiness and quality of life.

A few examples of priorities that can help drive our planning:

More time for our spouse

More time to care for aging parents

More time for children or grandchildren

More time to start a new business

More time to pursue a personal passion

A new schedule to enable volunteer work

More time to travel

Reduced work hours to simply create more downtime

More time to focus on exercise, diet, and physical health

More time to mentor young people or coach youth sports

This is, of course, a very personal thing, so we won't attempt to throw around rules here. The key is to make the shift, incrementally and in small steps, then reassess. Find your top priority, make adjustments in your schedule, and then assess progress—is the shift having the desired results? Do we in fact have more time to support our top priority(s)? Are we seeing progress in our quality of life, our happiness, our mental health? Are we in a better place than we were six months ago? Are we happier than we were a year ago? This constant assessment and adjustment process is healthy and very likely to bring us successful results over time. Even in the case of a momentary setback or lack of progress, we can adjust our approach before much time is lost. It is also possible that over time our goals and priorities may change, and we will have a number of experiences that can impact our assessment and reassessment of creating the right balance. This is all good stuff. The key is to be open-minded and honest in making our evaluations and then making the necessary course corrections. These is no secret here; it is simply a matter of being committed to evaluating progress. This mindset is a big step toward ensuring we find success.

Be patient and be committed, and you are likely to find the best path for you and your family to a new, more satisfying work/home balance.

CHAPTER 6

A NEW MODEL OF MENTORSHIP

Mentoring is a wonderful act of giving and a powerful influence for both the mentor and the individual benefitting from the experience and insights of a more senior professional. Many of us can remember a mentor who was instrumental in our early and mid-careers and likely had a lasting influence. The remarkable influences of a mentor never leave us and in many cases move us to pass along what help we can provide to others, those we will nurture to become the leaders of the future.

Mentoring is a timeless cycle of caring and supporting others, ultimately about giving back some of the priceless experience and knowledge we have gained over years of experience.

The importance of mentoring has never been greater, but what we will learn in the years ahead is that much of what we assume mentoring is, and is not, is changing forever.

A new model is here, not popular or well understood as of yet, but it will gain more visibility soon and then grow in the years ahead to become a vital new dimension to the traditional model of mentoring.

This new mentoring model now includes a new participant—intelligent technology.

Yes, intelligent technology will bring a new dimension to mentoring and will both benefit from people and contribute new value to people in a way never before possible for humanity or for technology. What we will explore in this chapter is a series of mentoring connections that include new combinations of people and technology. The process of mentoring is more important than ever, different in some ways but not losing the value. If anything, there is more value than ever to be unlocked when mentoring comes to life. We will explore the continued mentoring of people by people, as this remains the foundation of mentorship, but now we have two additional mentoring opportunities that will have a significant impact on every business over the next ten years. These new opportunities enable new learning and new contributions to be made where they were simply not possible before.

The first of these two new opportunities is people mentoring technology. Let's think about this for a moment. Technology needs the benefit of human experience and knowledge in order to learn and to learn the right things, to learn accurately, and to learn with context. It is certainly true that intelligent technology is voracious and lightning fast in its ability to learn, but in need of a source of the right information. Where there is content readily available to assist in the learning curve faced by intelligent technology, this won't be enough. The unique experience and expertise held by our people is a key source of information that must be transferred to technology. This will have a big impact on the effectiveness of automation and AI, to name a couple of examples of the technology that will play a key role in the future of the IT organization. Only through the mentoring of this technology by our key people and our domain experts can we dramatically accelerate the uptake of key information and put technology in a position to be successful, to take on critical work every day, and to ultimately offload our people to take on the innovation and customer-facing work that is so critical to the future of humanity and to the future of the IT organization.

The second of these new opportunities is technology mentoring technology. Yes, that is right, technology will mentor intelligent technology and show us that mentoring was created by humans and will continue to be advanced by humanity. But the mentoring of the future is not for people alone. It's not as simple as that, my friends. Technology will have a growing appetite for information, for insight, for context, and for key business rules, and this need for information will know no bounds. As our people experts are passing this information on to technology, and the technology begins to grow a broader and deeper understanding of how tasks are completed, how business processes are executed, and how business rules govern our work and decisions every day, the need will arise to pass this precious information along to other intelligent technology elements. This sharing model will mimic how the sharing happens among our people. But now we have technology participants in the mentoring process that through human mentoring have important information to share with other technology elements in need of this information. It becomes impractical and slow to assume that all mentoring must be conducted by people. That will simply no longer be the case in the next ten years, and the mentoring model will take a dramatic leap forward due to the simultaneous advancement of technology capabilities and technology needing this information in order to step up to an increased role in the business.

This new model of technology tutoring and guiding technology is deserving of a more in-depth discussion, and we will take this topic on in more detail later in the chapter.

PEOPLE FOR PEOPLE

This is where mentoring began, with a mentor guiding and helping a junior colleague to learn and better understand the many complexities of business. We use business as a primary example here, but mentoring can occur anywhere and in any discipline. The model is timeless, flexible, and adaptable. Now, as we face a new global economy, accelerating changes in technology, the continued evolution of the Internet, the influences of social media, and much more, we need the value and the relationships created through mentoring more than ever.

We make the point throughout the book that the future of IT is not about the remarkable advances in technology, as exciting as they might be. Our future is very much about people and the unique and priceless impact humanity will have on the new era of the IT organization as it unfolds before us now and in the next few years.

This continued dependency on people and the unmatched contribution they will make to the IT organization in the future reminds us yet again that an investment must be made in our people, both now and far into the future, and one highly cost-effective model for this investment is through a program of mentoring. If your organization has a structured mentoring program in place today, you are likely seeing an increased level of staff seniority and a higher level of IT maturity and performance. There is a clear relationship between the presence of a mentoring program and the ability of the organization to retain and develop staff. This is an example of a program that requires a relatively small cost and a relatively small commitment of time. All we need are a few good people willing to volunteer their time in mentoring a designated colleague, and the process then takes a natural course as both parties are likely to find the program rewarding and enjoyable.

This wonderful program is fully under our control and can be started quickly, with very little infrastructure or costs required. Some successful companies assign a rotation period of something like one year to the mentor and the apprentice, and then work with the good people of Human Resources to put the appropriate guidelines in place and to conduct checkpoints during the program and a review at the conclusion of the mentoring rotation. The structure can vary from company to company, but it is most effective when the process is kept simple, with very little administration, and the people are left with some flexibility in how they prefer to communicate and work together. A high percentage of the most successful market-leading companies of the past fifty years have utilized mentoring programs to develop young staff members into key contributors and leaders of the future.

Figure 6.1 People for People

As we face the transformation of the IT organization over the next decade and the new challenges placed on the teams of IT as the business dependency on technology and data continues to accelerate, we must leverage proven strategies where we can. And mentoring is a great example of remarkable potential value that is often overlooked in IT today.

Although the new mentoring model we discuss here is not limited to people, it does start with people working with people, and in doing so we are creating a foundation of learning and of building relationships that will carry us into the other two new dimensions of mentoring. However, without the knowledge and unique talents of our people, we will find that the domain expertise, experience, and understanding of key business rules that ultimately govern how a business operates every day will be missing.

This very human knowledge and understanding of precious context are the backbone of every organization.

This knowledge can only be cultivated over time and held by our people experts who are the original source of this priceless information. These same people then have a responsibility to the organization to share this information, thereby making it even more valuable and helping to ensure the future of the business will be strong. It is even possible for the next generation of experts to improve on the business rules, business processes, and how tasks are performed and how decisions are made. This improvement then makes the business better, making superior decisions more quickly and ultimately better serving customers and placing the business in a more competitive position in the marketplace.

All of these elements are connected and ultimately enabled by the precious knowledge held by the talented people of the IT organization. When we have mentors in place, this uptake of knowledge is greater and places each associate receiving the benefit of a mentor in a superior position to learn more, to learn more quickly, and to better perform their role in the organization.

While the chain of mentoring begins with people and the origin of all information today remains with our people, that is changing for the first time and will change dramatically over the next decade. We will look more closely at two examples of that change in the following sections.

A final comment and reminder—the participation of intelligent technology in the wonderful program of mentoring in no way weakens the role of people. This belief would be completely missing the point. The partnership of technology in mentoring will only strengthen the place of humanity in the process of learning and growing.

PEOPLE FOR TECHNOLOGY

There is a growing hunger within technology for information and for sources of knowledge to support and accelerate the learning process for the new generation of intelligent technology. AI and ML and other variants of intelligent technology today, as well as new generations of technology that will appear in the next few years, have a voracious appetite for information and for a better understanding of how decisions are made every day and how the organization operates. Why do people do what they do, what thought process supports this action, why are tasks performed as they are, how are business processes operated, and how are decisions ultimately made? What information is considered by the decision makers, what roles do instinct and intuition play, and what factors does a true expert consider that others might not?

Insights into these questions and many more are vital to the learning process and vital to the development of our leaders of the future. This process is timeless and has been in place since the beginning of business.

What is now new is that we are ready to welcome technology into the cycle of learning and to be the student of a mentor for the first time in earnest.

Intelligent technology is a remarkably capable learner, in most cases capable of learning far faster than a human teammate and virtually without limits. But in the beginning of this new cycle of learning that will dominate the next twenty years, this intelligent technology must have a reliable source for the necessary information. A source that can provide the context and business rules and business process definitions that are so valuable and the heartbeat of the business every day. Given this need, the only credible source we can turn to today is our people. Yes, our domain experts and our experienced leaders who understand how the business operates, how work gets done, and why decisions are made. Every good decision tells a story, and the thought processes for these decisions are full of critical considerations.

Our experts, talented contributors, and leaders will be mentoring people and growing our future experts and leaders. This comes first, but now this is not enough. Now our mentors must make time to mentor intelligent technology. This is an important extension of the new partnership between humanity and technology. It is vital because we expect so much of technology for the future and we are counting on intelligent technology to offload our key people in order to clear the way for new initiatives and a new set of priorities, but technology won't be ready to lend humanity this helping hand if technology is unable to learn and unable to access the required information. Technology can't learn what is required alone.

So now we have both humanity and technology in need of each other as never before—technology in need of the information only available in our domain experts and business leaders who understand every nuance of both how the business operates (think business rules) and the technical details that exist in every business, the nuts and bolts of the business that are understood by product experts, functional experts, consultants, support analysts, technologists, and others across the organization. This information must finds its way to the intelligent technology partners that will take on a large and growing segment of work that we will move to automation over the next decade. The projected standard for automation is to move the IT organization to 90% automated by the year 2025 (Ref 1), and this is only possible through many actions, including the mentoring of technology by these same experts we are in need of reassigning to other work activities.

It is beyond the scope of this discussion to explore exactly how our people will mentor intelligent technology, but this will be a process that looks very much like our people-to-people mentoring. Of course, small adjustments will be made to account for one of the parties being an automation engine, Bot, intelligent assistant, or some other form of intelligent technology, but the pattern and the content are the same.

We must capture and codify the business rules and content held by our experts and other experience-rich people and make this information available to the intelligent technology that will be performing a specific function. This might seem foreign to us today, but that won't last and will become natural in the next few years. It will become natural both out of necessity and because we are increasingly surrounded by technology. Just as Siri has helped condition our culture to work with AI/intelligent assistants in our personal lives and through the use of our smartphones, so will a new generation of business-focused AI elements in the next ten years. These intelligent assistants and automation engines will be optimized for business and specifically optimized for the IT organization. These technologies will be able to absorb and assimilate all information available for the IT organization, including every business rule, the definition of every task and how it is performed, every business process and how it is performed, along with exceptions and decision criteria for all operations. And this is just the beginning.

If you agree with this assessment and have come to similar conclusions, then you have likely begun the planning process and are well on your way. If this view makes you uncomfortable, seems too extreme, or you believe it will simply never happen, then I'm confident you will see the landscape of IT otherwise in the next few years and hope we have a chance to debate the fascinating evolution, preferably at a table in a fantastic restaurant.

After all, we can't change the future of IT on bad food and cheap wine!

We will close this discussion with a final point—this trajectory for technology should not at all seem sinister or something that will threaten our people. What we should recognize is that only humanity can assist technology in learning so much of what is uniquely held by our talented and experienced people, and technology needs humanity to fulfill its growing role in the IT organization. We should be generous with our time and our thoughts over the next decade or risk stunting the growth of technology.

It would not be misguided to view intelligent technology as a remarkably capable and intelligent infant—able to do so much but virtually helpless in the beginning and keenly in need of coaching, gentle guidance, encouragement, and tutoring and with this is able to grow quickly and virtually without limits.

TECHNOLOGY FOR TECHNOLOGY

We continue our discussion on mentoring with yet another fascinating dimension—that of technology mentoring technology. This will effectively represent the third generation of mentoring and one that will be with us for the next one hundred years and beyond. I mention the century mark because it will represent a new mentoring landscape where the tutoring of technology by technology will be the norm and not the exception, or a concept we will struggle to understand and appreciate.

A quick summary of the sequence here is as follows:

People mentoring people to nurture our people and domain experts

Technology joining the process and being mentored by people business experts and domain experts

Technology learning at an accelerated rate through the support of people, including interactive learning supported by interactions between people and technology

Technology reaching a critical mass of understanding and expertise through the mentoring of people with the necessary experience and context

Technology taking on specific roles in the organization to apply the depth of information learned from people mentors in order to gain experience and deeper contextual understanding

These technology partners then contribute to an expanded knowledge base and corporate databases through a new path of experience as operated by automation and AI elements.

As this technology-borne experience and knowledge builds and builds quickly, the senior technology elements step into mentoring roles much as their human counterparts would. This then creates a parallel path of technology mentoring technology alongside people mentoring people as well as technology.

In some cases as we will see, the sophistication and capability of technology increases including natural language skills, bring us to the point where we could see technology elements mentoring people.

The technology-teaching-people model will recognize that in some cases the technology could grow to become the "expert" in a given domain or on a specific subject matter.

This evolution and progression will happen at a remarkable rate. We can make the case that this sequence of learning through the new mentoring model will compress the learning cycle dramatically to the benefit of all—good for people, good for technology, and good for the business. That is a lot of good!

The sequence highlighted above only works, of course, when technology is able to take on the work we have envisioned for the new generation of automation and AI tools. This is just beginning to become reality. At the writing of this book in 2020, we have chat bots and automation engines in operations for many IT organizations, but this is just the beginning. Based on my own work with hundreds of IT organizations over the past decade, my estimate for the average level of automation in IT today is 20-30%. Some are lower, very few are higher. But, of course, this must change, and as another reminder, the 90/90 Rule calls for IT to be 90% automated by the year 2025.

This is an ambitious schedule for automation. We can include AI and all forms of intelligent technology in this category because it is capable of offloading our people from the high-volume, structured, and repetitive work and will give them the bandwidth to work on more strategic initiatives. Yes, we make this point again because it is so central to the evolution of the IT organization over the next decade. This brings us back to the strategy, and it certainly is a strategy, of technology mentoring technology. This process is not a nice-to-have; it is essential to support the learning curve of intelligent technology as it takes on a more prominent role in the typical IT organization in the near future. People alone simply won't be able to support the rapidly growing and voracious learning needs of intelligent technology as it is deployed in IT and across the business. The mentoring and learning process will certainly start with people as we described in the discussion on People for Technology, but will and must rapidly shift to the Technology for Technology model because people won't be able to keep up with the growing demands for information and learning on the part of technology as it takes on new roles.

We referenced earlier to the 20-30% automation level that exists in IT today.

To put this into perspective, we are expecting the presence of automation and AI to <u>effectively triple</u> over the next five years.

This is absolutely necessary, not optional, for many reasons. When we consider what this implies in terms of enabling and supporting the hundreds and then thousands of technology elements (a single automation or AI system/app) that will appear in IT over the next five years alone, it becomes clear the training/supporting/validating/coaching requirements for these elements are enormous and can't reasonably be met by people alone.

Our technology brothers and sisters must step up, and step up they will, to become the next generation of mentors for the junior technology elements in need of so much learning and guidance.

CHAPTER 7

IT LEADERSHIP

The leadership of the IT organization and the talented people of IT are not about IT alone. Nothing could be further from the truth.

This critical issue of leadership is about the future of the business, the success of the business, and the very survival of the organization. The reality of today's global marketplace and the digital economy is that technology and data are now strategic and are authentically the engines of the business. Those organizations that are able to connect business strategy with technology and to then leverage data strategically are the market leaders of the future.

This is the key to the future business—a business strategy that is in harmony with technology and data to the degree they are inseparable.

The organizations in any industry that harness the remarkable power of technology and enable technology and data to elevate and accelerate the business strategy are the market leaders of the future.

So, is it too late for most of us? Absolutely not!

Most of these new market leading organizations have not yet stepped forward, but the window for that to happen in most markets is the next decade. So the time is now for IT to lead, for IT to bring new solutions to the business, and for IT to bring the synergies between technology and the business strategy to light.

We can't wait and we certainly can't expect another organization to provide this leadership. The IT organization has the unique skills and expertise to bring business strategy and technology together. The people of IT are uniquely able to bring new and innovative solutions to the business, and never has this been more important than today. Every business, regardless of size, location, and industry, is in need of this connection, this blending of organizational and go-to-market strategy with the assets of technology, systems, and data.

Most of you will be nodding in agreement with this view. The key is that IT must step forward to fill this void and in doing so provide a new dimension of leadership in the business. Yes, I do understand this will be seen as controversial by many because it is simply not how IT is viewed today. How many leaders across the business today would describe the people of IT as leaders or proactive or aggressive? Very few, I would imagine, but that should not discourage us.

Great leadership can come from the most unlikely of sources, and this will be one such case.

The business is in dire need of this leadership, and this need will only grow over the next decade; in fact it will grow greatly and become a matter of the very survival of the business. The IT organization must take up the challenge. Having worked with hundreds of IT organizations of all shapes and sizes, I do appreciate that it will not be easy for the talented yet modest people of IT to see themselves in this light. It won't be natural and it will require an adjustment.

But we must recognize that this leadership in bringing technology and data together with the business strategy and the needs of customers does require this essential understanding of the remarkable complexity and nuances of technology, specifically intelligent technology and automation tools for today and the future. It is simply not possible to drive this convergence of the business with technology without this understanding.

With this realization we must ask where the technology, systems, infrastructure, and data understanding reside today? Where do these experts live in the organization?

Of course, they are the fabric of IT!

So, there is our unlikely but clear outcome: the best thinkers and the domain experts and the generally talented people of IT must now take up the challenge to fill this void and partner with the business and the rainmakers of every organization to lead us forward. Note that I'm not suggesting that the people of IT can go at this alone. That is certainly not the case—success is only possible through partnership with the business—but it is critical that we not wait. The IT organization must drive an outreach program, one that I will refer to many times throughout the book, and a program that will bring business leaders together to form cross-functional teams that will shape this new converged Business/Technology strategy and then tactics and operational plans to accelerate the full business into the future.

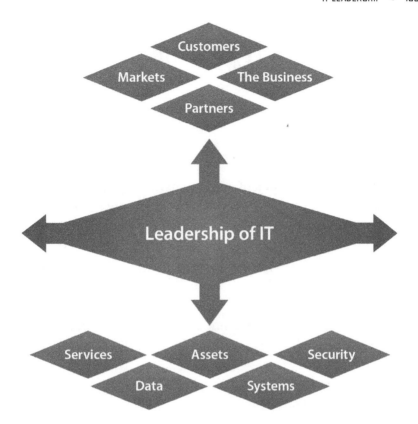

Figure 7.1 IT Leadership

Facilitation is a wonderful form of leadership, and so now is the time for IT to drive these discussions, to form the teams, to identify the business challenges that must be addressed, and to then shape the solutions that will determine a bright future for the business.

Although the specifics will vary from company to company, make no mistake that the time for the leadership of IT is now, and there is no substitute for the knowledge held in this organization. No substitute for the diverse skills of IT and no substitute for the unique balance of business understanding and deep technology and domain expertise that lives within the teams of IT.

It must be us, and the time must be now.

UNLIKELY LEADERSHIP EMERGES

In contemplating this idea of a new generation of leadership rising from within the IT organization, some of you might be a bit skeptical. Or perhaps *very* skeptical. That is only natural and to be expected; this idea that IT will step forward to lead the business into the future is not a commonly held belief and far from a popular opinion.

But that is okay and should not discourage us. A few doubters should not diminish our resolve to take on this challenge.

Any skeptics we encounter should not take away from the reality of the business currently being in need of leadership and the rapid rise of technology as a strategic enabler for every business, in every marketplace, of every size. This is an inescapable condition of every organization today. Few would question this rapidly expanding role of technology, and equally few would question the gaps in leadership that exist today in most businesses.

It is only on this point of IT stepping up to provide a critical element of the much-needed leadership and to help fill the leadership void that we begin to see a bigger number of doubters who are happy to explain why the future leaders can't possibly come from the IT organization.

Again, this is all fine, and just remember—skeptics never achieve anything great. Greatness is born of hope, optimism, and passion.

It's easy to doubt, and too easy to tell us all the reasons why a new idea just won't work. It's so easy to tell us why IT can't do this or can't do that.

These pessimists should only serve to make us more determined and to increase our energy for the work that lies ahead. Take this as a good thing, knowing there is nothing sweeter than proving the doubters wrong—they underestimated the good people of IT.

Now, enough time spent on the naysayers. We turn our attention to the task at hand—leading, enabling, and assisting in leading the business forward. In developing a new generation business strategy that is in harmony with technology and valuable corporate data. Because this leadership is not expected and requested of IT, we must be proactive and aggressive in taking the first steps forward.

This is an important point—IT must take the first steps. We can't wait for the organization to request that IT takes on this responsibility, and we can't wait for the other organizations to recognize the new leadership of IT. All of this will come in time, but in the beginning, we must take the initiative and begin to drive change. We have previously discussed an outreach program to be driven by IT, reaching out to the different lines of business and the key business owners across the organization to begin a series of discussions and evaluations that will ultimately drive widespread change.

Good people don't need a definitive charter in order to create real results. In the beginning, we only need a few basic goals and to start the right discussions with the right people, and naturally good things will begin to happen. Good people find a way. Initiating this process across the business and facilitating the right discussions and getting the right people involved begin to establish the new role of IT leadership. It will happen slowly in the beginning, and long-standing perceptions do take some time to overcome, but that is okay. A new perception of IT will take shape as we begin to form the small teams with the key business leaders and urge people across the organization, in every area, to participate in forming new strategies and bringing new solutions to the problems facing the business today.

Results will come and with these early results, the IT organization begins to emerge as a leader, as an agent of change.

As a quick reminder, a few of the key areas of focus IT will bring to the outreach and in creating a sense of direction for our cross-functional teams will include:

Improving the user experience for all business systems

Advancing the ability of users to serve themselves

Increasing the speed of performance of all business processes

Driving IT and the business to operate 24/7

Navigating IT and the business to 90% Automated Ops by 2025

Supporting all business use cases on mobile devices

Reducing the fulfillment time for key process processes by 90% before 2025

Of course, this is just the beginning, but this simple list of examples provides lots of opportunity and potentially lots of value back to the business. Remember, IT need not bring solutions to all these goals/challenges but rather should encourage and facilitate the formation of cross-functional teams, create a new level of awareness around the importance of innovation, and bring new and creative solutions to bear on real business problems.

The benefits of the IT organization creating this awareness, coordinating the start of the right discussions, and forming teams to work together on advancing the innovation that lives across the organization is a priceless service IT can provide to the full organization. What will naturally follow is the recognition of IT as a new and emerging leader for the future.

THE TIME IS NOW

Simply waiting because it is the easiest option in many cases can be dangerous and allow risks to take root in an organization.

Although there might be times when we can get away with waiting, with no clear or perceptible impact, this is not one of those times. The time has come for the IT organization to build plans where they might not exist today. This timing is important because so much is at stake, and waiting can begin to cause damage to an organization that will be difficult if not impossible to recover from.

Some planning is necessary, but it should be simple and quick. The planning itself can't become a barrier to launching into action and beginning to provide the guidance and leadership that is so needed today. What we have seen work best in cases where action is needed and delays and waiting must be avoided is a quick, iterative approach that streamlines the planning process. With the ability to perform short work phases and then quickly and informally evaluate results, the pressure to get everything just right in the planning phase is lifted. This simple principle has a presence in both Lean and Agile, and while new frameworks deserve some degree of credit for advancements in how we work every day, there is a good dose of common sense here too.

The thing to keep in mind is this—when quick action is needed, any value associated with a longer, structured, detailed planning process is far smaller than the value that will come through mobilizing our actions quickly and being guided by a simple plan, knowing the process will account for regular intervals of reviews, evaluations of results, and then making the resulting updates to the current plans. This latter model is recommended to avoid any further delays and to launch our teams into the new model of working where we have cross-functional teams assembled to go after the key business challenges impacting the business today. Every business has these and of course they are not the same from organization to organization, but there are many natural similarities.

In fact, this model of acting fast and planning for frequent reviews/ assessments and adjustments to the plan is not natural for IT. It is not how we have worked in the past, but now is the perfect time to create a new model and form new habits.

It won't be easy, and we should recognize that up front lest we get discouraged when challenges or resistance are encountered in the beginning. Shifting our way of working, shifting our lifestyle effectively, will be an adjustment and won't be comfortable. But that is okay and is to be expected. We will get through these setbacks quickly, and truly every day will be a little better.

But the key is to get started now. Make these changes now, make it clear that we are committed to working differently now. Set these expectations up front and be clear, and we will be amazed at how quickly people will adjust and want to help. It is natural for most people, and even more natural for our best people who have a spirit of help and a spirit of teamwork running through all they do. There is an element of cultural change present in this approach because acting quickly and moving fast is not natural for the IT organization. We have been accused of being slow to act, of being reactive and overly methodical. It is possible to overcome these long-standing perceptions, but it will take a little time and some action on our part.

Nothing makes a statement quite like action.

It can help to communicate the plans of IT and share our aggressive goals. But this alone won't begin to change perceptions. Perhaps a little, but no more.

However, when we begin to act proactively and more aggressively, to act quickly and move fast, people will take notice.

Then, with the actions that follow, perceptions do begin to change and the word spreads fast that "something is going on in IT." This can be fun and it can bring us energy to continue on our journey of change, and to provide the leadership, including leading by example, that is so needed in IT and in the business today.

If we make some mistakes, that is okay. Even this simple mindset begins to change the culture of IT.

Acting now and moving fast becomes the priority, and making a few mistakes is an acceptable risk. This will be a foreign concept for many IT organizations, but that is to be expected and should not block us from acting and therefore beginning to make changes to the culture of IT. It is a powerful force of change to free our teams to move fast and make it clear we are willing to trade velocity and a few mistakes along the way for moving slowly and making fewer mistakes. This tradeoff recognizes that slowness and inaction are a form of poison to IT that we can no longer accept. In the beginning it might be necessary to reinforce this idea and encourage our teams to pick up the pace. This is a big change, and lots of reinforcement from management and IT leadership will be necessary to change behaviors and break old habits.

But our people will take to it quickly, because moving fast and acting more aggressively will be a natural to many of our people and will be a welcome change. Time for change and time to act differently—acting now, moving with speed, being aggressive in all we do, taking some risk, and IT emerges as a much-needed leader in the business. But remember, this starts within IT. We get our own house in order by changing our own behaviors and then take it to the business and have some fun along the way.

PROACTIVE ACTION BEGETS LEADERSHIP

Continuing with our previous discussion, let's build on this idea of action, proactive action, and IT driving forward initiatives we know are important to the future of the business. This new mindset will be ignoring, for many good reasons, the traditional boundaries and stereotypes that exist across the business. One of the best reasons we need to ignore the traditional models and all that come with them is that it creates too much indecision and too much waiting. Too many people assuming somebody else will take the actions needed and too many delays as a result. In the current global economy, speed is strategic, and speed creates competitive advantage.

Waiting is dangerous, and systemic waiting, caution, and slowness can threaten and ultimately kill a business.

Speed is powerful, speed is empowering, speed is sexy, and speed is appealing to customers.

The inroads of speed in the organization today lead back to IT. Business is conducted over email, with mobile phones, on mobile devices, with CRM systems, with ERP systems, and much more. All of these systems are enabled and then managed by IT, and as such it is inescapable that IT lies squarely on the path to speed. We can take this a step forward and conclude reasonably that the best way to bring speed into the business is through IT initiatives that specifically look to maximize speed every day.

Speed in every task that is performed

Speed in every business process

Speed of performance in every system

24/7 access to all business systems

The ability to self-service virtually all business actions

No waiting to begin a business process

Leveraging AI and Intelligent Technology to increase speed

Commitment to improving every user experience

Meeting or exceeding the 90/90 (1) rule

Speed is a good example, but it is not the only example of where we need the proactive action of IT. The IT organization needs this action, and the business needs it equally if not more so. With IT taking proactive action and not waiting ever, in any form, we see a shower of benefits across the business. Everything begins to happen faster. Our people are more productive, and customers are happier. Happier customers in turn then make our people happier and more confident, which brings yet more goodness to the business.

Why all this talk about speed in a discussion on leadership? That is a great question and brings us to a reminder that the teams that drive real change into the business become our leaders of the future. When positive change begins to happen, and speed is a great example of positive change, all the people touched by this change will want to be part of the movement and will respond to the people and teams that are driving a new way of working. This is role-modeling which naturally evolves into leadership. People are drawn to other people who are doing what they know is right and needed for the future of the business.

This is the recommended path for IT—begin to drive the necessary changes now and for the greater good of both IT and the business, because these changes are critically needed and far overdue. We can't wait for an official charter, and we can't wait for a formal and structured apparatus to be formed. Waiting will kill us. And so the right way forward for IT is to identify a few of the key strategic initiatives that will shape the future of the business and to launch actions around these initiatives, driven by small cross-functional teams, and to do that now.

Drive innovation and fresh thinking across IT, and these actions will quickly carry over into the business. The momentum will not stop. What is missing today is the start, the beginning of the actions and people and teams willing to do something new and to take some risks and drive change. This change must happen and will happen; there can be no question on this point. There is too much seismic change happening in the global marketplace and in global culture to ignore the need for change in every business. If we accept that change must happen, it is needed now, and we can and should start with a few simple actions, then the people of IT can take up this challenge to be the agents of change so needed in the business today.

A few simple actions taken now will quickly grow and naturally pull good people into the effort. The energy and passion will spread quickly. Soon, results will begin to come and the impact grows more quickly and the circles of influence and excitement grow equally.

With this remarkably simple yet powerful wave of change and the proactive actions that were the catalyst for the change, the recognition of IT leadership naturally grows and to a large degree is unavoidable because the recognition will always come back to the people who started it all. This is a wonderful and lasting shift in the perception of IT across the business and within every team.

CHAPTER 8

LEVERAGING PEOPLE

There is nothing more important to the future of the IT organization and to the future of the business than the ability of the greater
organization to strategically and thoughtfully leverage our people.
Our people are uniquely talented and yet we have not utilized them
as such in the forty-year history of IT. In many cases, how we have
assigned our people is quite the opposite, and traditionally they
have been deployed on tactical and highly repetitive work. The normal grind of IT has consumed the large majority of our time. This
is all perfectly understandable when we consider the reactive and
survival-first culture of many IT organizations since we began to
call this organization and its talented and dedicated people IT. This
is simply part of our culture and born of the realities and demands
placed on the teams of IT every day.

That is the journey we have traveled, but the journey that lies
ahead will be very different. Now we are moving through a new beginning, and it is happening fast, much faster than we might understand. For many reasons, including the partnership of intelligent
technology, we have our first opportunity to recalibrate the traditional model. This realignment of IT will include many new priorities, but at the heart of what will drive the new IT agenda will be:

Obsession with the customer

Innovation in everything we do

Leveraging our people in strategic roles

Building a new culture for IT

Designing for Speed and Automation in everything we do

These priorities should not be a complete surprise as they appear in many of our discussions throughout the book. They permeate virtually all that we will do in IT for the next decade and beyond.

In fact, if we focus on but a few of these core strategies, we can't go too far wrong.

Even where we don't specifically call out the human element of a priority, it is always there. The people of the IT organization are our future, not the technology, and we should never be confused on this point. People will drive our new relationship with the customer, people are uniquely able to create new innovative solutions, automation frees our people to focus on the uniquely human tasks that need our attention, and so it goes in bringing us back to our uniquely talented people.

Invest in our people and we will find success. Invest in the people of IT and innovation will follow. Nurture happy and motivated people in IT, and we will create happy and loyal customers for the future. Invest in growing leaders in IT for the future, and we will create the future leaders of the business. All of these things are connected, inseparably joined even when it might not appear so.

Look a little more closely and we will find the thread of humanity and our people running through everything that is important to us.

A NEW PARADIGM FOR PEOPLE

The transformation and reshaping of IT will cause us to look differently at our people. Always there, and always a part of the IT organization, we have taken our people for granted for far too long. As is usually the case with an oversight, there are good reasons for this and all very understandable, but now we must expect more of ourselves and more of our people. The leadership of IT must form a new paradigm for the role of people in the future of IT. As these roles come to life, it will forever change our perception of people as humanity, and we'll have a greater appreciation of specific people as they step into new roles and expand existing roles.

This will be an exciting journey over the next decade—we are defining the window for IT transformation and the many changes that come with this seismic shift across the organization, as a decade. Ten years might seem long but they will disappear quickly, will give us adequate time to make the meaningful changes that lie ahead of us, but at the same time the years will certainly fly by!

The time of writing for this book is 2020, so we look forward to the year 2030, by which time most of the changes have been made. Those organizations that are unwilling or unable to make these changes and embrace a new paradigm are likely to fade away and become a new generation of business that dies due to the new way of thinking and working every day.

A critical element of the changes we will see in this decade of IT rebirth is how we think about our people. Traditionally, we have thought of the jobs that must be done and then which of our people we can assign to the jobs. This was all very simple, somewhat necessary, and thoroughly tactical. It was a very basic system of fitting people into roles and for the coverage of tasks with only the shallowest degree of thought on how people are matched up with work. Remember, it has been a model of survival for the past ten years in the IT organization. We did not dare look beyond the here and now and what was required to complete our work today. To continue with the inertia of this model, when new hires were made, they were normally driven by a backfill for an existing job. We continued the existing model and created a new generation of workers who did essentially what was done by their predecessors. And so it went.

The new paradigm will be very different. The new thought process will look to not simply fill the needs to complete current tasks and business processes but rather will seek to staff the strategic initiatives first and with the right people. This will be a thoughtful and critical process and take some time, and that time will be well spent. We must get this part right or all other assignments won't matter. The strategic activities are what will drive the engine of IT and are critical to all of IT and to all of the business. This process was rarely performed in the past due to the burden the tactical work and the high-volume tasks put on the organization. This work stole so much of our oxygen and made it difficult to see the future and all but impossible to find a better way.

So, what has changed? An excellent question that we need to explore.

It begins with an increased appreciation for our people and staffing our strategic work, the initiatives that will have a real impact on IT and the business. This new appreciation starts with IT leadership, rolls into IT management, and then becomes part of the mindset for every staff member in IT. We must constantly reinforce how important this challenge is—matching the right people in IT with the high-impact work that will strengthen our future.

This is essentially a vote of confidence in our people, their future, and the future of the IT organization.

A critical message that all our people must hear.

We can't emphasize our areas of strategic focus too often, so just a few examples of this discussion:

> *Customer-facing projects*
>
> *Improvement of the user experience for every system*
>
> *Speed improvement initiatives*
>
> *Business owner outreach*
>
> *Innovation-focused teams*
>
> *New communication models*

Of course there are many more, but these are some great examples of where our best people can be assigned to better leverage humanity and build a stronger future for the IT organization.

In a few words, the paradigm shift is moving from asking the question:

> What work is due today and who can we assign to get it done?

To a new question:

> What are our strategic initiatives and who are the best people to staff this strategic work?

This second question is then supported with a subsequent action following the assignments to the strategic projects, which is the action plan for the automation of the majority of the remaining work given it did not qualify for the strategic initiative short-list and therefore must be considered tactical, operational work. And a full 90% of this work must be automated by the year 2025. This push to automation is important because it brings the many benefits of automation, including speed, scalability, 24/7 operations, and agility, but even more importantly it offloads our talented people, thus enabling them to be assigned to the high-impact initiatives that will change the future of IT. We are reminded yet again of this important synergy between automation and the new focus for our people that creates a new paradigm for precious humanity.

This simple and powerful relationship is a key pillar in the future of IT.

PRICELESS SKILLS

One of the many wonders, and there are many, of humanity are the unique and remarkable skills only found among our people. Only possible and only available through our people are skills including but far from limited to:

Advanced problem-solving

Verbal communications

Sense of humor

Determination

Passion

Empathy

Friendship

Creativity

Loyalty

Trust

Teamwork

An infinite range of emotions

Affinity for negotiations

This simple set of examples is remarkable in its own right, but only the very beginning of what our people can offer. In scanning this list of skills, we are reminded of the miracle that is the human machine, the countless unique skills held by our people, and their ability to adapt and grow over time in wonderful and unpredictable ways.

In thinking about these skills for a few minutes, we can also map one or more to the strategic work we must ensure our people are assigned to over the next decade.

This decade is our window for transformation, and as such,

we can't afford to lose any time in assigning the right people with the right skills to the work that only our people can drive and the very work that will change the future of IT and of the business.

This connection of people to strategic work is how we need to begin any staffing discussion and every organizational planning process. It is just too important to not get this right. These thoughtful assignments are among the most important decisions IT leadership and IT managers will make over the next ten years. Why? Because if we don't have the right people on the customer-facing, innovation, and business outreach activities that occur every day, we won't make the changes to IT that are so critical. We can't transform IT and the business working in the same ways and with the same people and with the same reactive/tactical mindset and manner every day.

Figure 8.1 The Skills of Humanity

The remarkable changes we can and must drive from within IT are only possible when we put our talented people in the right roles at the right time, and set these teams up for success. So much is at stake. It all begins with awareness and focus and building the right teams with the right charter. Then, give them some room to work and prepare to be amazed. When we put passionate and talented people in a position to thrive and grow, it is highly likely they will do exactly that: find a way to deliver and to exceed our highest expectations and accomplish remarkable things. Real results and real change can happen, but only when we give our wonderful people the chance.

These is no magic here, just capable people working together. We only need to give them a chance. And for this discussion we are focused on applying these priceless and unique skills not yet present in intelligent technology to the strategic projects that only our people can drive to success.

Yes, AI and Automation have certainly come a long way and are far more capable than these technologies were just a short five years ago. But make no mistake, the ability to solve highly complex and dynamic problems, the ability to show empathy, the ability to form a sense of unity in teams, and the ability to negotiate with a client are just a few examples of the skills that must be tapped in our people. It is only in our people that we find these answers.

Will AI and a new generation of intelligent technology display these remarkable skills in the future? Perhaps. If so, will it be twenty years or thirty years or even fifty years before intelligent technology can match these same skills held by our people today? It is hard to say, and a fun debate to have over dinner when we have a chance. What we do know is that only our people have these talents on full display today, and so we move forward with what we have, knowing we can achieve hugely impactful results now, and just in time for the business when it needs us most.

But it all begins with the recognition and appreciation of the priceless skills held by our people and then assigning those staff members to the strategic projects. This seems simple enough, but in the day-to-day demands of IT, amongst the changing priorities and the pressure to deliver results now, it's not as easy as it might seem to make these assignments. It's not easy to give our people even a little time to make progress on shaping creative solutions to real business problems, or working on a customer-facing initiative, or improving the user experience for one of the growing number of systems our employees and our customers rely on every day.

Starting small can make a big difference and be less overwhelming.

This can be a couple of our talented people assigned to just one of our strategic projects, giving them the opportunity to shift their focus away from the daily deliverables and daily operational work. Although a small and contained effort, never underestimate the impact of making the commitment and showing the conviction to make a change in how we work. The people we assign to these small teams will notice, and their many peers and teammates will notice as well. All will be buoyed by this clear message that IT is investing in our talented people, and together, we will build a stronger, brighter, and more exciting future.

EVERYTHING MUST BE BETTER

People are a wonderful and sometimes miraculous source of change. Humanity has an innate ability to find a better way. A pull to improve, to find something better, to do more with less effort—it can only come from our people. This is a timeless desire that rises up from within people, but the time is right for this drive, for this energy for getting better, because it is needed by the IT organization and by the business.

To start, we must recognize that what must be better, what must improve, is nothing less than everything. Nothing is good enough today and nothing can be out of bounds in our search to improve. Make everything simpler; make all that we do and deliver better.

Sometimes improvements come in very small, almost invisible steps, and sometimes we are able to take a large and dizzying leap forward.

Both are equally important. Our journey to being great can't be about the big breakthroughs alone. If anything, the small improvements can be more important, and the sum of which over time may very well exceed those large leaps. Never underestimate the importance of getting just a bit better, of doing things just a little smarter, of finding a way to save just a few seconds on the average task. The mindset we want to encourage is of curiosity, a healthy desire to understand first how we do our work today and why we do what we do. Then we seek to understand how we can simplify the necessary work and how we can do everything better. It helps to keep in mind that we will almost always find ways to improve something that we study carefully. This can be a simple task, a business process, or a complex system.

The key is the desire to seek the better way and to think. Simply thinking about any problem and how we can get better is so powerful. It is remarkable how often people work without seeing, and toil away every day without thinking. When we don't take the time to ask why or to think, then we are virtually assured of not getting better. But when we do take the time to ask questions and understand the how and why of everything we do, we are already well on our way to finding a better result, of finding a way to get better in the small and large things we do every day. Achieving great results is far more about a willingness to ask questions, a desire to find a better and smarter way of working, and to find that next step in getting better in everything we do. Where that desire exists, there is very likely to be a successful outcome regardless of the challenge. Conversely, where the curiosity is missing and the desire is not there, we are assured of getting the same results over and over and over.

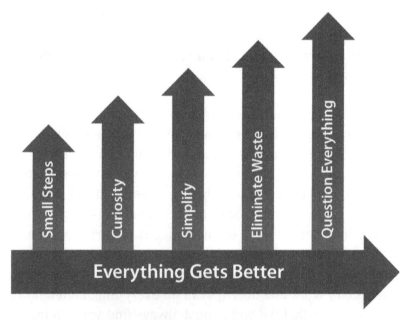

Figure 8.2 Everything Gets Better

This fundamental desire to get better and the willingness to ask questions and find even the smallest improvements is very much a cultural change. Never underestimate the power of culture and in creating a better way of working, of encouraging our people to ask those transformative questions of "how" and "why" and "what-if." When we begin to ask these questions and begin to truly commit to improving, that is an unstoppable force for good.

And once these healthy changes in our culture have begun—the curiosity and the willingness to ask questions and the desire to get a little better in everything we do—this all builds a wonderful spirit that is contiguous and runs quickly through every part of the IT organization. Many of the most powerful formulas are the most simple, so let's summarize these connected ideas:

> *A desire to improve in all we do*

> *Even the smallest of improvements is important and should be celebrated*

> *Encourage curiosity*

> *Ask lots of questions*

> *It is critical to understand "why" and "how" for everything that occurs in IT*

> *Seek to simplify everything*

> *Eliminate waste wherever we find it*

> *Encourage brainstorming to find new solutions*

> *Nothing is off-limits and everything is worthy of improving*

Remember that some of the biggest improvements come to us in the most unlikely of ways and places, so it is critical to leave behind any old boundaries and assumptions. This stuff can block us from finding the next critical improvement and sometimes the most critical advancements.

Never forget this simple strategy and never discourage the healthy curiosity and questions that sow the seeds of real improvements in everything we do.

CHAPTER 9

THE INNOVATION ENGINE

At the heart of our charter for the rebirth of IT over the next decade is an unwavering commitment to innovation. Innovation brings value to the IT organization, to the business, and to the many customers who will benefit from every creative solution to existing challenges and to the future improvements that will be made to prevent challenges and frustrations that have yet to impact the business.

Think of this as innovation being the best possible prevention for anything that can present a risk to the business in the future.

Frequently not considered to be in the charter of the IT of the past, we must now move past that and make Innovation not just a part of IT priorities, but a core focus—an initiative that demands the staffing of our very best and most creative people. Innovation will draw people in, and the excitement will build when we begin to show a commitment to this new investment of capital and people.

Certainly, innovation as a reaction to an existing issue in the business is in itself a powerful elixir to what ails the business,

but even better is innovation that will be proactive and prevent future limitations and challenges from occurring.

This is the model we now strive for—looking ahead at the trajectory of the business and crafting creative solutions that anticipate future needs and deliver flexible, agile, adaptable, and scalable solutions that will stand the test of time.

A wonderful element of innovation is a never-ending source of opportunity and inspiration. The process never stops, and therefore it helps to think of innovation as less of a project and more as a lifestyle.

Once the commitment to innovation has been made, it changes everything. We see everything around us through a different lens.

This is far from a grind or a burden, but rather a source of excitement and of challenge. We challenge ourselves in IT to seek the business problems of the day and take them on. By taking them on we mean taking a systematic approach to better understanding the problem, defining the basic variables that govern the problem, and then launching into our process for creative brainstorming and problem-solving. This is precisely where we leverage the "engine" we referred to in the chapter title.

The engine is a structured and consistent approach to innovating. We can't just wing it. This is far too important to accept risk. We are constantly tweaking and improving the engine based on experience and based on new successes and, in particular, new failures. The improvement of the engine never stops. It is now far more important to move quickly and take some acceptable risk, versus let caution and fear of failure paralyze us. This is common and in many ways part of the traditional culture of IT. Playing it safe and continuing to work the way we have always worked will all but ensure our failure to meet the new challenges of the future. Playing it safe and simply reacting to the deliverables requested of us will also ensure IT will not transform or emerge as a leader for the future— both of which are unacceptable outcomes. We must transform IT and build a new model in virtually every area. In doing so we lift

IT up to be a leader of the business into the future. Both of these outcomes are only possible with innovation.

Innovation is fundamental to the success of any business in the future and critical to market leadership. Taking this further, innovation is best originating from the heartbeat of technology and data—within the IT organization. Certainly this is not the only origin for innovation but in many ways is the best and most authentic launching pad for innovation over the next ten years, what will be a decade of new and exciting solutions to what slows us, what frustrates us, and what keeps us from being at our best every day both in business and in life.

Innovation has a unique and unmatched ability to show us a new future.

IT ALL STARTS WITH AN IDEA

Never underestimate the value and impact of a simple idea—a new and original thought—none of which should be dismissed because the next idea could be the one the business needs to catapult the organization forward. We want and desperately need crazy ideas, a completely new and never-before-considered approach. These ideas have the ability to change everything. A remarkable ability of our people is the creative and unexpected shaping of a new approach to a daunting business problem. A solution that we all would feel was right there in front of us, but it took the right person at the right time with the right idea to show us the light. These ideas are truly priceless and can come at any time from any place across the organization. A key to innovation is recognizing the value of these ideas and creating the opportunity for the thought and then the shaping and sharing of the idea that springs forth from careful reflection.

Simply having a little time to think is remarkably empowering to our people and to innovation.

Innovation can only start with new ideas. When the idea comes, it launches the innovation process and innovation engine into action. This is a chain of events that can only take place with an idea. The idea is a priceless catalyst that our organization can rally around, drive the discussions and reviews and evaluations that make up the work that occurs as part of innovation.

A great idea creates unlimited energy.

Innovation includes a business process that guides us from the beginning of the innovation sequence of events through to the final realization of a new solution that can only become reality through this process. Because the business process of innovation can only come to life with an idea, it's critical that we value these ideas and encourage our people, who are the one and only source of these ideas today. The best IT organizations of the future will be those that are able to create and grow a fertile culture for the ideas that make innovation possible. Without the right value being attached to new ideas and without the ability to advance new ideas into investigation, prototyping, and ultimately the ability to bring the best new ideas through to fruition in whatever form that might take, innovation will not exist.

The leadership of IT and the managers responsible for the development of the people and teams in their charge must recognize just how important innovation and the new ideas that make innovation possible are to the very survival of the IT organization and the business. The chain of events for new ideas and innovation looks something like this:

Communication that reinforces IT has the charter to bring new solutions to the business

These new solutions must come from a proactive IT

The creation of forums to share new ideas

The review, discussion, and vetting of these new ideas

The ability to identify the most promising ideas

A defined process to develop selected ideas—referred to here as prototyping

A further extended process to invest in piloting the best prototypes

Planning for the investment in successful pilots

Productization of successful pilots to create production systems

Recognition and reward for those people who originated the seed idea

Constant support and encouragement for this innovation chain of actions

People will take notice and be inspired when innovation happens; they will want to be part of the process and bring future ideas up for review. Remember, this needs to be simple and will always include some forum for brainstorming and discussion. Creating a schedule for the forum in which ideas are shared and reviewed and discussed is important because it can be the key step in both demonstrating a commitment to innovation and giving the best ideas a chance to find the light and move forward. The forums for ideas can be simple and informal—over coffee in a morning forum, or during a midday lunch break, or at the end of the week on a Friday afternoon when people are a little more upbeat and energized. All of these have been used to great success by some of the leading IT organizations around the world. The key common denominator is simply creating the forum or some equivalent structure to ensure there is a regular opportunity to discuss key business problems and brainstorm possible solutions. These discussions should be inclusive and welcoming to anybody who wants to join and has ideas. I can assure you that sometimes the best ideas come from the least expected of sources, so don't assume that the next great idea that will result in an exciting innovation will come from the smartest member of the team or the most experienced or most senior person in IT. Sometimes yes, but this will not always be the case. We can't design a forum or a process that makes it difficult to participate or that is unwelcoming to new input and crazy ideas.

We all need to welcome those new and completely fresh, unexpected ideas! They help forge the path to our future.

MAKE TIME

Time is precious, and never has that been more clear than today. We have fewer resources in IT and more projects competing for our time.

With this reality it's not easy to make time for innovation or the other strategic projects that are so important. This is essentially the challenge—our strategic investments are more important than ever and our resources are more limited than ever and in particular those very resources that are uniquely qualified to drive innovation, customer engagement, business outreach, and the other top-tier projects that will change the future of IT and the future of our business.

The simple but anything-but-easy reality is that nothing happens with innovation and establishing the remarkable machine we need for the future if we are not able to make the time and free our people from the shackles of the daily tactical and operational work. So, we are left with facing the challenge of making the time. This is the first step. Regardless of what is happening in the daily flow of IT—and in the crazy world around us—we must make the time for innovation. Even the smallest of steps can make a remarkable difference. We can start small, with only a little time, and even the smallest of steps begins to change everything. Only the smallest of opportunities can blossom into a momentum that will build over time.

A few examples of how we can start small with innovation:

Assign a small team of two to three people to look at a key business problem and propose solutions.

Create a new brainstorming forum to exchange ideas.

Identify a customer frustration and allocate a small block of time to investigate—this can then grow over time, but getting started is the key.

Follow up on the feedback from key business owners on user experience.

Structure a weekly allocation of time to focus on innovation, with one or a few people.

A full-time assignment for a single person is always best, but if this is not possible, we can start with a half day or one day per week.

Remember, even a few hours per week will make a difference.

Even the smallest of time allowances sends a message to all of IT and to the business. Never underestimate the signal this work will send and then the encouragement and energy that will rise from the smallest of efforts. Small initiatives will reinforce the priority of innovation, and our people certainly understand the load IT is under and the natural challenges that are created in finding the time to invest in innovation. This fosters respect and a support for leadership when we find this time and all people appreciate the priority behind innovation.

We only need to get started.

For those organizations that have already made the commitment and found some time, the next step is finding a little more. We start with a little, and then we find a little more, and then a little more. This is the reality of the journey—one small step at a time and soon we will have made remarkable progress that is far greater than the small steps that have been taken, because a full understanding of progress is far greater and far bigger. Our measure of progress must include a recognition of the optimism and passion and energy we have created by unleashing the creative energies of our people.

Passion and energy are unstoppable and give our people a sense that anything is possible.

Our organization and our leadership are committed to our people and believe in our ability to build a better future for IT and for our business. This all springs from a modest investment in innovation and the other sister strategic projects that will shape a more dynamic business that is able to create happy and loyal customers.

We should never lose sight of the fact that innovation is not simply about innovating—innovation is about a stronger and more competitive organization that can better service customers and in doing so build customers who are loyal for many years. It is a remarkably strong pull that is irresistible for today and for the future. Customers are naturally drawn to an energetic business with passionate people. It's something everybody wants to be part of. When we reflect on how this culture is created, it is virtually always connected to innovation and the search for creative solutions. These elements are all connected—true innovation always stands clear from all other products or services in a given market, and the people who propel the engine for innovation are more committed and more passionate about the organization and about our customers. Conversely, an organization that fails to innovate will be creating a culture of mediocrity, a culture of low energy, a culture that fails to be excited about the future and one that fails to have the sense of optimism and energy that is virtually without exception characteristic of market leaders.

Innovation changes the mindset of our people and changes our culture from the inside out. The only other single thing I have seen with an equal capacity to transform a culture and transform the IT organization is the customer connection, an authentic passion for customer success.

While the humanity of IT must balance many priorities for the future of our business, innovation and customer success stand at the top of what is most dear to us.

RECOGNITION AND REWARD

We're all naturally drawn to and inspired by recognition. When we receive praise for our efforts, even a modest amount, it makes a big difference in our attitude and the commitment we make every day to our role and our company.

Aligning recognition and reward to the projects that hold the highest priorities in the organization is a great way to motivate our people and hold their attention on the work that will make the biggest difference for the future. A consistent plan for recognition and reward is a great driver for ongoing success for innovation and should be part of any plan to help ensure the success we need to have on the strategic initiatives of IT. Any short-list of the top projects for IT must include innovation.

Note that we include both recognition and reward in this discussion. They go together to create a powerful result in our people. Recognition can come from management or from our peers and teammates and serves to bring attention to a job well done, a successful task or project, an important milestone. Any accomplishment deserves only a few minutes of our time to reinforce what is most important to us. Recognition can be for anything, and there is no achievement too small to make the time for a thank-you on behalf of all the people in the IT organization and the business. There should be no boundaries here. This can include IT recognizing the business in addition to the fundamental recognition for the people of IT solely. A good program of recognition should include a mix of individual recognition as well as for teams. This can serve to further reinforce the importance of teamwork and team success. A good team can accomplish anything—truly an unstoppable force in an organization and an agent of change for a culture. A culture that includes teams that are working together on small and big projects alike and are recognized when milestones are met and key deliverables are achieved is a wonderful thing to behold and a key part of virtually every healthy culture regardless of market and organization size.

There is simply no case where good teamwork won't make a difference.

Although recognition alone is powerful, it is best when in concert with an appropriate reward process. Rewards can come in many forms and serve to reinforce the good work that is being done and complement recognition. Issuing rewards is an opportunity to be creative. Cash is always good, but we are not limited to cash bonuses alone, although bonuses should have a place in every rewards program. A few options for rewards, each of which is very effective:

Gift cards

Cash bonus

Paid time off

A thoughtful gift that lines up with a personal passion

Trophy, plaque, or similar ornamental reward

Company branded jewelry or clothing that is unique to the program

Packaged vacation

There are no limits to the fun and meaningful things we can do with rewards. Each will have an immediate and lasting impact on the team or individual receiving the reward, and it will be something remembered.

I have yet to see a successful IT organization that did not appreciate the importance of recognition and reward and have a program
in place that fosters this commitment. The form and content of
these programs vary a great deal, but they are always there as a
necessary ingredient in IT being successful and in retaining the key
people who make a difference every day.

We simply can't expect IT to perform as a whole if we are not able to
retain our key people and build tenure across our staff. Remember,
tenure is always a good indicator of the overall health of the IT organization. When average tenure is in the two- to three-year range,
it will likely reflect an IT organization that has broad performance
challenges. Yes, there can be exceptions, but this is typically the
case. However, when we see average tenure in the six- to ten-year
range, we normally find a strong IT organization that is reliable and
delivering consistently to the needs of the business. This begs the
question: What if our organization is somewhere in between? To
find the answer we need to look a little more closely. If the tenure
is increasing over the past few years, then the organization is on
the right track and making strides toward building a stronger IT. If,
however, the tenure is dropping consistently over the past years,
it is a sign of risk and requires immediate attention, including a
commitment to a recognition and reward program. The decline of
staff tenure in the IT organization is often a leading indicator of
challenges that must be addressed quickly and systemically before
they have an impact on overall business performance.

If we are looking for a few quick wins with regard to staff morale,
a simple program for improved staff recognition and reward is a
great place to start and will never disappoint.

CREATE THE PLATFORM

Innovation simply can't happen without a foundation, a platform designed to nurture what is most important to make innovation possible. The right platform is not just a physical thing—the platform is a combination of a few critical things that together form a fertile foundation for the ongoing creation of new solutions.

A few examples of the critical components of the innovation platform include:

A culture that values innovation

Dedicated resources assigned to innovation

A proving ground for validating elements of future innovative solutions

Forums for open discussion and brainstorming

A system for recognition and rewards

Communication with the business to identify key business challenges

Influx of new technologies that directly support innovation

Your organization might have additional needs, but these can be considered a core set of requirements to advance innovation. Note that not all of these elements are necessary to build some momentum around innovation. If your organization lacks a commitment to innovation in the IT organization today, only a few of these elements in place can begin to make a big difference in innovation. The key is to build the platform and recognize the multiple dimensions that are required, each complementing the others.

It all begins with the commitment to innovation. When this commitment exists, the people of IT will find a way.

The pull of innovation is powerful and it is fun.

There is nothing more exciting than shaping a new and creative solution to a real business problem that has slowed the business and then enjoying the benefits that come quickly when the new solution is put into place. This then builds a sense of confidence in the organization, and commitment grows stronger, thereby increasing the likelihood we will find the next innovative solution. And so it goes.

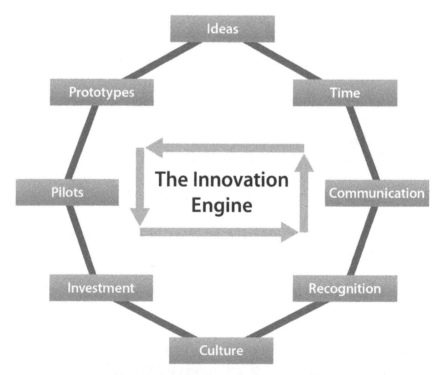

Figure 9.1 The Innovation Engine

Even the most advanced and admired IT organizations, those we assume have always been great, have not always been strong. At some point in their history, they, too, made a commitment to innovation and took those critical first steps. There is no magic here, just an appetite for and the willingness to do the hard work necessary to build our platform and get started.

Starting the work is the hardest part, and it can be anything that gets us started.

Virtually any first step is a good first step—it can be with culture, with creating a brainstorming forum, in assigning a small team to identify the business problems we will go after, or any of the others we show above and possibly a first step that you identify as making the most sense for your organization. That is great. We only need to get started and remarkable things will happen. It makes sense to perform an assessment of the current organization and evaluate where the biggest holes exist today. Put another way—what is the biggest obstacle to creating the innovation platform and bringing innovation to life? Every organization is different, so this will very much be personalized to your organization and require a fresh and critical look at the current state of things. It will give us a sense of the best place to start, and it's always a good idea to go after the most daunting obstacle. If that is not possible, then identify an element of the platform that can be executed quickly and with low risk, and this then becomes our natural first step.

Examples I've seen be successful as a first step in building our precious innovation platform would be assigning a small team to shape a solution to a particularly high-profile business problem or the formation of the brainstorming forum at which ideas are welcomed with regard to how we make the systems of IT better, how we improve the user experience, or how we address any of the known business challenges at the time. Any of these areas are fair game and of course any others that are brought to the forum. If the forum is overrun with potential targets and some focus is called for, then ground rules can be defined and serve to help define priorities and provide some structure going forward. These examples might be a good fit for helping your organization get started in building the platform. Or your team can identify a different area. Remember, there are simply no wrong answers here. All that matters is communicating the importance of innovation to the future of the IT organization, a commitment to building a platform that makes sense for your organization, including some but not necessarily all of the elements we presented earlier, and then the discipline and fortitude to stick with the commitment for the months and then years necessary to begin yielding real innovative solutions for customers and for the business, backed up by a growing pipeline of new and raw solutions that will be evaluated and nurtured to ultimately yield the new solutions of the future.

Remember, every innovation in IT and the business is priceless and capable of changing the lives of our employees and our customers.

Never underestimate the impact of the next innovation IT brings to the business.

CHAPTER 10

QUALITY OF LIFE

So much of what we discuss throughout the book—both directly and indirectly connected to the humanity of the IT organization, the wonderful people of IT—is capable of enhancing the quality of life offered in IT both today and into the future.

Without a better quality of life, and ultimately without an excellent quality of life in IT, the future of IT will be threatened. The endless hard work of today combined with growing levels of stress and greater demands from our responsibilities outside work, all create an unsustainable pace and load on our lives. While this can be said of many jobs and can be a fair commentary on our world today, this is particularly true for those people in the IT organization. The acceleration of technology, the value of data, and the always-on expectations on business have all collided to greatly accelerate the crushing load placed on the shoulders of the dedicated people of IT.

This simply must stop, and we are called to reset the quality of life model.

This must happen now, and with the transformation of IT, the rebirth of IT, we have a fantastic opportunity to do exactly that—to reassess everything around how we plan and execute work in the IT organization effective immediately.

This all begins with putting our people at the front and center of how we build the future of IT. Of course, this is complemented by a new "inside-out" lens for how we view everything, and there is a natural connection between our people and our customers. This is the inside and the outside, but these entities become one when we embrace a new mindset.

As we move forward and embrace this new beginning for IT, planning changes and improvements to the IT organization both today and into the future, we ask the following questions:

> *How do we improve the quality of life for the people of IT?*

> *How does this decision improve or decrease our quality of life?*

> *What is the biggest challenge to our quality of life today?*

> *What single thing can we do to improve the quality of life in IT?*

> *Does a mechanism exist today for feedback on quality of life?*

> *Do managers regularly discuss quality of life with their teams?*

These simple questions and others you can add for your organization will grow the awareness of quality of life as a central issue in the future of IT and will change the discussion and expectations going forward.

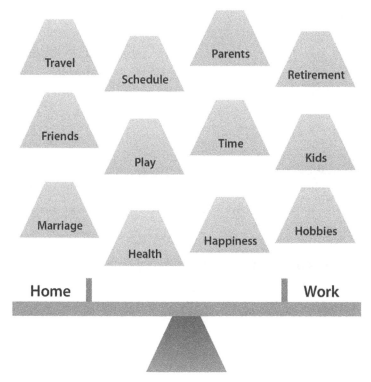

Figure 10.1 Quality of Life

This is essential—the time has come for us to change our priorities and create or change the discussion around quality of life. A new sense of awareness has the power to further transform IT.

It should not be lost on us that an improved quality of life for our people and a better quality of life across the IT organization have many direct and significant benefits to the overall business, including:

Happier employees

More productive employees

More passionate and energetic workers

Longer employee tenure

Employees who are advocates for the business

Improved customer service

Growing customer satisfaction

Cultivating an improved quality of life for all the people of IT is a great example of an investment that pays back to us in many ways and is good for everybody. This captures a powerful and limitless set of synergies.

If this is not worthy of our attention, what is?

THIS IS EVERYTHING

Improving the quality of life for the people of IT is not just another thing, not just another initiative. It is far bigger than this, and we need to look a little more deeply. We are called to look at this issue more thoughtfully because there is so much at work here. Quality of life has not been a focus of IT in the past, and it was not a matter of not caring about our people, because that was certainly not the case. No leader in IT whom I've had the pleasure of working with did not care about the people on their teams. This is not a case of negligence or leadership lacking respect for their people.

This is a matter of creating a new focus and a new priority that specifically focuses on quality of life. There is a big difference between caring for the well-being of our teams and the individuals who make up our teams, but not taking explicit measures to improve quality of life in everything we do—and making a commitment to a consistent and designed investment of time and resource toward improving the quality of life for all the people in IT. Remember, this is a multifaceted issue that pays back to the management of IT, to the business, and even to our customers in many ways. This return on our investment if you will is generated through the many benefits of a happier and healthier workforce. As quality of life increases, so much more grows right along with it. We can say that an index of worker happiness, productivity, loyalty, passion, and engagement grows in lock-step with quality of life.

These factors are inseparable.

Likewise, if we see a decline in the quality of life for our people across the IT organization, we are all but assured of seeing a decline in employee tenure, employee morale, and worker productivity, and the metrics we can track around customer satisfaction will suffer in concert.

This brings us to the clear conclusion that a focus on and investment in quality of life for our people is central to improving so many of the things that are vital to the future of IT and the future of the business. We must elevate this need to the top tier of our priorities for the future, and this focus brings us immediate and long-term benefits that are remarkable and without limit. Even the critical priorities we have discussed throughout the book—including Innovation, Culture, and Customer Engagement for example—will directly benefit from an improved quality of life in the IT organization.

So, what does that look like? A few examples of key elements of quality of life include:

Creative compensation plans

Health benefits

Flexible work schedule

Employee development plans

Mentoring programs

Employee recognition

Team celebrations

Fun employee activities

A diverse workforce

Access to customers

Strong company branding

Active cross-functional teams

It's fun to think about how we can improve quality of life for the people of IT. A good exercise is to ask ourselves: What would make me happier and more productive in my current role and in the future? This makes it more personal and makes the discussion easier to carry forward. No doubt you can think of several good ideas very quickly because this is in fact a very personal issue that directly impacts us as individuals and our family. What is important to our spouse? What can help us provide for our children? What enables us to commit another five or ten years to the company? What makes a difference in us feeling a sense of pride in the company we work for? These are but a few examples of the strong emotions we create when quality of life improves.

With this very brief examination of quality of life in the IT organization, it is easy to see why it must be elevated to the top tier of priorities for what we accomplish in the future transformation of IT. It would not be much of an exaggeration to say that if we work together to dramatically improve the quality of life of the many talented people across the IT organization, we have in this single action also been successful in transforming IT. Yes, there are other matters that demand our attention, and it's not quite that simple, but it bears considering that few other things we can act on will have the impact of improving quality of life in all we do.

HAPPY IS ALWAYS BETTER

The power of happy is remarkable and natural. Happy is also simple. Everybody knows that a happy moment lifts us up and makes anything possible. And a happy day enables us to be at our best. Although in the past we have not often found a discussion around "happy" to be a normal part of the dialogue that happens in IT every day, that must now change. This will change because we find that happiness is so fundamental to building a strong future for the IT organization. The leadership of IT must understand that we can't meet the many goals we have laid out before us if we are not able to build and sustain a happy workforce.

We have chosen to focus on this concept of "happy" here for many reasons, not the least of which is because this is clearly a big departure from the traditional agenda for the IT organization. Realize that the agenda for IT over the past forty years has been all about efficiency, cost savings, productivity metrics, and doing more with less. Each year it seems that the workload on IT continues to grow while our budgets and resources continue to be under pressure and in most cases are flat to down. We simply didn't think about the happiness factor across our teams—how could we find the time to think about people being happy? Many people would think the very idea to be crazy and to have no place in the world of IT.

But despite this idea of "happy" being overlooked by many, it is a powerful force that can transform an organization. Just a few of the many benefits of happy employees:

Higher productivity

Better customer service

Longer tenure

Stronger future managers

Higher energy

Healthier lives

More passion

Better teammates

Advocates for the business

Better mentors

Like many other unconventional ideas we consider and address throughout the book, overlooking the happy factor must change.

We can no longer ignore the toll of an unhappy and overstressed workforce.

The good news is that the goal of "happy" is not as difficult to reach as we might think. For virtually every IT organization, it is within reach. A few small things along with awareness make a big difference. It is remarkable the opportunities we will find when we begin to sincerely search for ways to improve the happiness of our people. What we will discover at the same time is that our people will immediately recognize the effort and appreciate the recognition and effort to advance the happiness factor among the workforce and with this the overall quality of life. These things go hand in hand, although the actions around happiness can be a little easier to implement and a bit narrower.

In many cases a few small things can have an immediate impact on happiness. Some examples include:

Flexibility in work hours

A few planned employee outings

Team coffee or lunch meetings

An inexpensive gift or gift card to a favorite retailer

Informal recognition of a job well done or milestone hit

A day of vacation award

Note that at the time of this writing in 2020 and during the time of COVID-19, any of these ideas can be implemented virtually or in the traditional in-person model. There remains uncertainty around what the working model for 2021 and beyond will be, but these basic concepts will continue to apply and, if anything, "happy" becomes more important than ever. Certainly, the demands on IT and the stress of our jobs have not decreased in the least and in some cases have grown.

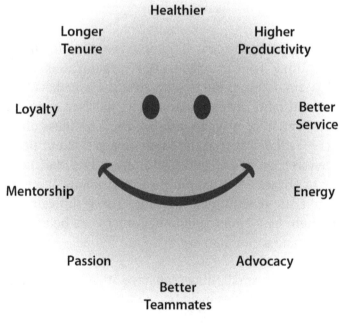

Figure 10.2 Happy Is Better

When we accept the importance of a happy workforce and begin to look around for opportunities to move the joy of our teams forward, we will discover opportunities everywhere. In most cases these ideas are not expensive. They just take some interest and a little time. It bears repeating that with these small investments we get an immediate payback on the action itself, but we get perhaps an even bigger payback over time as our people recognize the efforts of leadership, management, or teammates and sincerely appreciate these efforts and then feel like part of the process and want to pass it on to others. This creates a powerful chain of good and giving that further accelerates our motion toward a happier and more productive workforce.

Happy is truly always better, and all people are naturally drawn to those around us who are happy. Happy brings optimism and positive energy, and with these powerful tonics, anything is possible and every day is more fun and more fulfilling.

A NEW BALANCE

The good people of IT are always seeking to find the right balance; whether we are aware of this or not, it is always there. We seek a balance between our life outside work and the demands of our personal lives, and it doesn't stop there. We also seek a balance between the many priorities facing us in every role across the IT organization. These balances are natural and always present. It is simply not possible to complete all the work placed before us every day, and with this we are left to make many decisions about where we put our precious time. In this discussion we will address the idea of balance in the context of our job and these many competing priorities, and we will address the balance of work and home.

Both balances are critical and both are changing.

We begin with the balance of the many needs vying for our time in the job we perform for the IT organization. The demands of the business on IT continue to grow, and there will never be enough time to complete the limitless requests that come our way. And so we are called to view these requests a little differently and to create a new and more effective filter, a simple model for triage that guides where we put our precious time.

Each organization will vary, but in all cases the teams of IT face tactical work and strategic work requests every day. The traditional balance of IT was along the lines of first-come-first-served or to complete the work that caused us the least pain, or in some cases to complete the work that is impacting the organization the most, today. Right now.

This is all completely understandable and a natural way of working for traditional IT. However, this model will not enable us to meet our goals for the transformation of IT over the next five to ten years, and in understanding this, we must also recognize we have a responsibility to forge a new model. This new model need only be simple and consistent so it's easy to apply every day. A simple outline for this model looks something like this:

Make a distinction between tactical and strategic work.

Establish a fixed envelope of time that limits tactical work each day.

Commit to a block of time each day reserved for strategic projects, which include innovation, customer engagement, and the like. The block of time for strategic projects can be anything, but no less than one hour.

Set a quarterly target for increasing the block of time for strategic work.

Ensure management and IT leadership fully support the model.

Rigorously enforce the strategic and tactical work boundaries.

Recognize that some operational requests might take longer to complete.

We will leave it to you to shape the model to your organization, including the details of how this can be implemented. But the fundamental and simple principle here that must be protected is the careful structuring of time allocation every day to the standard tactical and operational work along with an investment in strategic projects.

This is so important because the inertia that exists in the IT organization today will never allow us to escape the demands of operational work if we don't perform a reset, the creation of a new set of ground rules for how the time of IT is managed and how we view the priorities of the organization. Simple yes, but easy no. This is very much an exercise in making a commitment to change the model and create a new balance. The truth is that without this commitment, we will continue to be consumed by the countless tactical demands pushed into the IT organization every day. Without this commitment, the opportunity for IT to innovate, to move close to the customer, to drive an outreach to the business and create better alignment, and to change the culture of IT for the future will all remain a dream, and we will have failed ourselves and the business.

A perfect and clear opportunity to reset this balance will never come, and so it is left to us to make the change and to do whatever it takes to make the new model a reality.

We will find we have many supporters when this change begins. Our very best people in IT and the leaders across the business will recognize the value here and applaud the efforts of IT to fundamentally change how we work every day and begin to make the vision of a more proactive and a more strategic IT a reality. This has been our dream for many years, and the time has come for us to make the shift.

The good news is that this is fully under our control. In creating this new balance, anything becomes possible. We have taken an enormous step toward a new future for the IT organization and in reaching the potential that is so important to energize and accelerate every part of the business.

The second balance we will discuss is that between the demands of our job and the demands of our lives outside work—the life we live on our personal time and with our family. Whether you are single, or married, or married with kids, there is a timeless struggle between what we are called to do in our jobs and the time we give to our life outside the job.

For most people, a job is necessary to provide for the basic necessities of life. The job tends to dominate our lifestyle, and what time is left over is then given to our family, as small or large as it might be.

As with the balance of our demands at work, we must also reset the balance between the job and our personal time. These things are related and we should undertake both with no more delays. Most people recognize that one or both of these balances is not right today, and they are similar—the demands of tactical work versus strategic work in our jobs is very much like the demands of our job versus the demands of our life outside work.

Together, these two adjustments hold the key to a happier and more fulfilling future.

In balancing how we manage our time at work, we are in many ways preparing ourselves for the corresponding balance of time between job and home—these are not so different at many levels and are directly on the path to a higher quality of life and the immeasurable satisfaction that comes with "making things right." This is a great time to keep things simple, and once again we turn to a simple checklist to help guide the way for the choices we make in the new work versus home balance as follows:

> *Being honest with ourselves is a key. Brutally honest.*

> *What few things are we missing in our personal lives?*

> *Validate each will bring us a better quality of life and is achievable.*

> *What does it take to bring these thing(s) to reality?*

> *Focus on what is under our control.*

Let go of what is not under our control.

Validate the necessary investment of time and resource.

Redirect the necessary investment from work, incrementally.

Take small steps and take care not to fully sabotage our jobs.

Revalidate the necessary investment of time and resource.

Periodically revalidate the few "happiness factors."

First things first.

Share our plans with those closest to us and ask for help.

This is very much a lifestyle change, and the people who have made this change are rarely disappointed and will only wonder why they did not make the commitment sooner. This is a time, as with every big action and decision in our lives, to work hard and pray hard. An element of faith makes anything possible and can remove obstacles that can otherwise seem overwhelming.

It also helps to communicate our plans with those closest to us and ask for feedback. These friends, family members, and coworkers can help us adjust course if needed, and can offer a helping hand when needed the most. This is a remarkable source of encouragement and energy that is critical to our new life balance success, but these people can't help us if they don't know. Be brutally honest with these people as we have been with ourselves, and this will help bring us success, whatever that might be.

You can do it. Don't let anything or anyone stop you.

CHAPTER 11

THE NEW WORKFORCE

The workforce of the IT organization is changing as never before. This change will take small steps and large leaps as we move into the future, and it is absolutely necessary in order to ensure we can meet the challenges of IT transformation while at the same time meeting the evolving needs of the business. The typical IT organization of today is not equipped to meet the demands of the future. It would be foolish to expect a successful transformation of IT and to successfully equip IT for the many new demands of the future with the same skills, the same makeup of people, the same culture, and the same manner of working. This is a fool's errand and should not be entertained. Any planning for the future of IT should include a design for the right workforce to carry our organization into the future.

When IT goes to the business and when the business comes to IT, we must have the culture, skills, and people to deliver—and, of course, to surprise many people along the way, which will make the journey a bit more fun. We will discover that our beloved IT organization will be doubted and stereotyped and underestimated time and time again. We should not let this discourage us. No way. If anything, we should use those doubters of IT as motivation and a source of inspiration and energy to do the work that will be required of us.

Strong and confident people love a challenge and welcome the

opportunity to prove skeptics wrong— these are the people we
want as our teammates in the future of IT.

This is yet another journey within the journey—another remarkable layer to the complex remaking of the IT organization.

The new workforce will include new skills, new approaches, new
talents, more diversity, and much more. In some cases the new
skills will come through new hires or transfers from other organizations in the business, and in some cases the necessary skills
will come from training and development programs within the IT
organization. Under the right conditions, this is a wise investment
in our people. It provides the opportunity for our people to continue forward in the IT organization and to build a stronger future
by acquiring or enhancing existing skills, moving into new roles,
and taking on new challenges. The development of people already
working in IT can't be the sole source of the new skills we need for
the future, but it can be an effective complement to the new people
we will bring into the organization and a valuable improvement to
the culture of IT. This sends a strong message that will be appreciated by all of our people and helps to build a sense of loyalty and
comradery across our teams. The first place we look for what we
need in the future is within our own. The talented and dedicated
people of IT should never be underestimated.

The new workforce is built step by step, person by person, and
each small step forward is important. Never underestimate the
impact a single person can have on an organization. This is how
we build a new workforce, and with these new skills and energy,
the people around us are energized and influenced without limits.
These single steps can be the training of an existing staff member
in IT who will be part of a new role in the organization; it can be
the transfer of a person from another part of the business into the
IT organization; or it can be the backfill of a staff departure with a
new hire with the necessary skills and mindset. Speaking of mindset and attitude, both are vital and certainly no less important than

the skills themselves. We vitally need people with the right energy, with the right optimism in the IT organization of the future. Great things are only accomplished with optimism and energy.

We need to bring some much-needed swagger to the IT organization.

Confidence is a powerful enabler for what faces us in the future. We need to create the feeling that *we are IT and no organization has more talented and capable people than we do. We are up to the challenge, whatever that might be*...

The IT organization will be ready no doubt, but only with the workforce that is equipped for both continuing the traditional duties of IT, which are in fact timeless, as well as meeting the new challenges associated with innovation, customer engagement, a new teamwork model, partnering with the business, redefining the speed of business, enabling 24/7 operations across the organization, and much more. These new priorities offer us a glimpse into where our future investments must come and how and where we must extend the experience, knowledge, and skills across IT. Creative skills, customer-facing skills, budget planning, communications, and business analyst skills are just a few examples of where we will look to expand the talents of IT. Remember, this won't happen quickly, because the right people and the right skills are not easy to find.

But they can be found and nurtured over time, so be patient and selective. This is our future.

BREAK THE MODEL

So much is assumed today about the IT organization—both what the organization is and what the organization is not. The business and in some cases the world around us will try to put IT into a traditional box and keep us there. So, it is left to us to make a shift and to break away from these conventions and create a new IT organization and workforce that can be described with many words, including:

Diverse

Creative

Energetic

Passionate

Communicative

Risk-taking

Proactive

Aggressive

Youthful

Innovative

Committed

Talented

Note this outline is very different than how IT would likely be described today, and we should be honest with ourselves about the perceptions that exist, including in our own house of the IT organization. But that is okay and we now take this on as a challenge and have fun in that we will surprise a lot of people on our journey.

The model is not changed overnight, and we certainly can't overcome long-standing perceptions quickly. It will take some time. We can only do it with measured steps and by ensuring that we develop the talents of our existing people, double down on the skills we need for the future, and at the same time thoughtfully bring new people into the organization with the right skills and, perhaps even more importantly, with the right attitude. Back to our list above, we must have passionate, energetic, and creative people to drive the future of the IT organization. This mindset makes anything possible.

With energy and passion, greatness can happen.

The mix of the right skills with the right attitude is an important one. We can't shape a new workforce and shatter the old IT model without both in place. Skill alone won't get us there, and great attitude is powerful, but it must be enabled with the right skills in place. This once again reminds us that we are called to be focused on both and in nurturing the people we have with regard to mindset and skillset while taking every opportunity for a backfill or a new hire in IT to fit the right profile. Glance at the list of attributes shown above, add a few of your own, and we use this template to qualify every person who will come into the IT organization over the next ten years. This is the decade of change, the decade of IT transformation. It won't be easy, but it is fully under our control and very much within our reach.

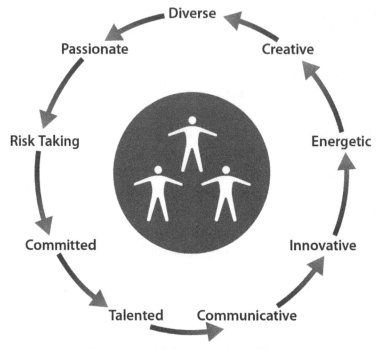

Figure 11.1 The New Workforce

By growing the right mindset and the right set of skills across IT, we are equipping the organization to do the work that is required of us for the future. This is very much a journey to break the model and shape the new IT. It helps to think of this as a journey in that it will bring us the patience necessary to recognize that the new workforce can only be built one step at a time and with commitment and discipline. There will be good days and there will be bad days, but we continue to forge ahead regardless. Then, gradually over time the new model begins to emerge as we see new behaviors emerge across IT, and with the new behavior we see new talents rise that make us able to take on new initiatives and influence the business like never before.

We need to remember that when we get discouraged, the very survival of the IT organization is at stake and, in many cases, the very survival of the business as well. We won't make the case again here, but there is much evidence to support the position that the business of the future can't succeed without a strong IT organization. There is simply too much dependence on technology and data for any business, regardless of market. And if the stewards of these valuable corporate assets are not up to the task, the business will suffer greatly and to the extent that the very survival of the business can be questioned. This all brings us back to the importance of breaking the model and creating the new culture and the new workforce that are uniquely able to remake the IT organization and propel the business into the future.

There is no magic here. We build the model one person at a time, one skill at a time, and lifted up by the energy and passion of our good people.

DIVERSITY

We have touched on the topic of diversity in IT a few times in the previous chapters, but we will give it more attention here because this simple point is much deeper and more important than one might think at first glance. It is fair to say the IT organization has not been especially diverse in the past. And this is being kind. This is simply part of the history for IT, and there are many reasons for the makeup of the traditional IT organization. But like other factors we explore throughout the book, we can't face the future with an IT organization that lacks true diversity.

To be a bit more clear, diversity for the IT workforce extends to include the following considerations:

Diversity of age

Diversity of ethnicity

Diversity of skills

Diversity of work experience

Diversity of interests

Diversity of talents

Diversity of styles

What we are seeking in the IT organization of the future, the one that will emerge from the transformation of IT, is a truly diverse organization in every respect. No one single category above is enough—we must thoughtfully design, implement, and nurture diversity in every regard.

This is not just about diversity for the sake of diversity. The value goes far deeper than we might appreciate at first.

Diversity will make us stronger, make us more united, lift us to better decisions, enable us to form more effective teams, create a more energized workforce, enhance leadership, sustain the full needs of our employees, and create an organization of more character with more balanced leadership. These few examples highlight—and this is only the beginning—just how diversity, when it begins to grow, will make us better and stronger in every respect. As yet another journey within the journey, the work on diversity is never fully completed. This is a commitment we make, a core value for our culture, and we then work to improve diversity every day. This work will further serve to develop a new generation of leaders in IT who bring with them an appreciation of and a commitment to diversity and its continued growth.

This will then continue to strengthen the IT organization and cultivate the thinkers and leaders we need for the transformation facing us today, and the challenges of IT and the business for the future. We, together, are effectively remaking IT for the benefit of IT today and also for the future benefit of the business.

It should not be overlooked that a more diverse workforce creates a more diverse and stronger culture, and this very issue, the culture of IT, might be most in need of change. As the forces of change come to culture, we then begin to see improved performance against our key initiatives, including innovation, customer engagement, business outreach, and improving the agility and speed of IT. Note that each of these initiatives brings tremendous benefits to the IT organization and then immediately to the business.

The business can't effectively innovate without the leadership of IT.

What does this have to do with diversity? The precious diversity of skills, talents, and experience across IT is exactly what is required in order to elevate the effectiveness of our innovation efforts. We can't simply say "Go" and expect IT to launch into innovation projects that will bring us new and creative solutions. Our investments in diversity will bring us the people and the capabilities necessary to make innovation successful, now and for the future.

Another dimension to authentic diversity is leadership. Diversity brings us lasting leadership. And while this will begin in IT—because our own organization might be where diversity is needed most and a domain that is fully under our control—as diversity begins to grow, we will create an unstoppable influence over the business. Our efforts will be noticed and the IT organization will be role modeling what the future of business will look like and begin to show the results and benefits that come from diversity. This will build some leadership momentum for IT, and at the same time, we are strengthening the performance of IT every day in virtually every category. We will establish IT as a go-to organization and a recognized leader for the business and an influencer and trusted advisor for clients.

There is no limit to the benefits, both large and small, that come to us with diversity. It's another reminder that there is more than meets the eye for many of our investments in IT that might seem tactical or operational on the surface. But with a little thought, we recognize there is a wonderful web of strategic benefits that come to IT and to the business when we make the commitment to these initiatives, to a new lifestyle in many respects, with true diversity being a rich and exciting example.

OLD AND NEW

With all this talk about making changes across IT and the necessary transformation that lies ahead of us, it would be a mistake to assume that we are changing everything about IT and the IT workforce. "Out it must all go" is not a cry we want our teams to hear!

There is much that is good in IT today, and just as it is important that we are willing to make changes and start anew in some cases, there are other cases where we must protect what is working today and what is good about IT. The very best we have in IT today is just as important to the future as the new attitudes, strategies, processes, and culture we will thoughtfully shape for the future.

We must embrace the idea that Old and New together make us much stronger than relying exclusively on what is New.

There is a critical balance here between Old and New that we must find:

> *Experienced people and new people*

> *Existing ideas and new ideas*

> *Proven tools and new tools*

> *Legacy systems and new systems*

> *New ideas for simplifying work*

Old but reliable processes with new processes

Proven solutions with new solutions

As we turn a critical eye to virtually everything in IT, it's important that we are equally committed to protecting what is old and good as we are to changing out waste, what does not work, what is complex, and what slows us down. This is the balance we must find. And just as keeping the status quo and protecting everything old will surely cause us to fail, we are equally at risk in believing that everything must be new and that nothing in place today can go forward into the future. We challenge ourselves and our teammates to be open-minded and objective about all the systems, business processes, and assumptions we will review in the months ahead, and we must be equally clear on what should be taken forward and what must be purged from IT and replaced with a superior solution that fits our model for the future.

In the context of this discussion on our workforce, we turn our attention back to the culture and our people. One great example of Old and New is teaming our most senior people with our most junior people in IT. This is the idea of Old and New in action. This unlikely combination creates some wonderful and unlikely results. And in virtually every case we will discover that this combination is very productive and able to create solutions that would otherwise be out of reach. The "old" in this equation is our grizzled and hardened people who have in some cases been with the IT organization for twenty to thirty years. These workers have a priceless understanding of how things work, why they work the way they do, and many such insights that are all but invisible to a new member of IT. The older and more experienced member of the team will also remember many examples of successes and failures for virtually every case and how each came about. We should also appreciate that the most experienced members of IT have seen a lot and with this unique perspective sometimes tend to be a bit cautious and skeptical of new changes and new ideas. This is all okay too and some of what we need from the veterans of the IT organization.

The "new" in this equation represents the new workers who are now joining the IT organization. These are in many cases a twenty-something group of workers who are joining IT immediately following school or soon thereafter as one of their first jobs. These younger workers have a different way of looking at just about everything. They are naturally more comfortable with technology, are natural users of social media, have a very simple model for communicating through non-voice channels, and have a keen understanding of how to get things done simply and efficiently. It should also be noted that these workers are somewhat impatient, and I mean that here to be a very desirable quality. They are not afraid to question everything or ask why a process or a system works the way it does.

In browsing through these differences, we begin to realize that the "old" approach has some merits as does the "new" perspective. In fact, having very different views can create something unique, something very strong and balanced when they work together. These differing views round out the other, and enable a team staffed with both the new and the old to find new approaches and new solutions that would otherwise be impossible or invisible if we only had one of these two perspectives represented on a team or a project.

In recognizing the opportunity to find creative solutions to current business challenges by forming teams that bring together the "new" and the "old," we need to shift our thinking away from what potentially can be avoiding these pairings to embracing teams staffed with both the new and the old. Going a step further, we need to consciously pursue bringing together our most experienced people with our newest and least experienced people,

and then stand back and watch amazing things emerge from where before we might have least expected it.

CHAPTER 12

THE SOUL OF A COMPANY

One precious thing, perhaps the most precious thing of all, that humanity can uniquely bring to a business is the heart, the spirit, the very soul of the organization. This should not be underestimated—the great companies in any market have a very distinct identity, a set of values, a virtual soul that governs everything that happens across the company every day.

This identity and soul must and can only come from the people of a company.

Humanity is uniquely able to craft this wonderful mosaic of ideas and emotions that together provide a guiding light for the future.

The shaping of the soul of the company happens both naturally, and should be cultivated within our culture and guided by leadership. It is a series of informal and formal discussions that happen across the organization and serve to build a set of core principles or values that our people can identify with and use as a foundation to create a stronger sense of unity and a common purpose. This is a wonderful thing when it happens, and those companies that have this strong sense of values and a corporate identity will invariably find success. These are the companies that are the market leaders of today and into the future.

For the rest of the organizations that have not found this identity, that don't yet fully understand what they are and what they want to be, it's not too late. In fact, most companies fall into this category, and so does the corresponding IT organization. And so once again we find ourselves in IT in a position to lead ourselves forward and in doing so lead the business forward. Our teams across IT should find our collective soul: what we want to be as an organization and how we get there. What do we stand for? How will we make a difference in the world today? What does it take to be proud of our company and of the job we are doing? This is an endless series of questions we can pose in order to jumpstart the right discussions and find our way. We should see this as a "fun" discussion to have and an exciting topic to take forward. These questions and the search for answers they bring will weave into the fabric of our culture a new sense of coming together—a new sense of how we get better and pick each other up when we stumble on the journey. As we undertake the rebirth of IT, there will be good days and bad days, and that is okay. This is to be expected. We help each other through this, and our sense of corporate identity, our collective soul, is exactly what makes us strong enough to meet and overcome the challenges that lie ahead.

Figure 12.1 The Soul of a Company

Please don't mistake the use of the terms "corporate" or "company" to assume this discussion only applies to organizations of a certain size or in a limited number of markets. That is not the case. The same ideas and goals apply to a small company of five people as much as a global organization of 500,000. The need for a soul and identity applies equally to schools, government, retail, manufacturing, technology, and every other market we can put a name to.

This idea of a soul in a company is for all of us, and calls us to be something bigger and better, something more meaningful that we can only be together and could never achieve alone.

A powerful, limitless, and remarkable idea such as this can only be born in and carried forward by our people, the wonderful and miraculous humanity of IT.

PASSION

Passion is a remarkable force in the culture of any organization. It would not be a stretch to call passion an unsurpassed quality that lives in the people of any team looking to build a stronger and more successful future. Passion has countless direct and indirect benefits:

Passion creates energy.

Passion generates confidence.

Passion supports commitment.

Passion directly enables happiness.

Passion is attractive to others.

Passion is a natural enabler of Leadership.

Passion fuels strong teams.

Passion is normally accompanied by Integrity.

Passion is often followed by success.

Passion tends to nurture optimism.

Passion generates speed in all our actions.

Passion encourages decisiveness.

Passion is naturally proactive.

Passion helps to shape a culture.

Passion overcomes obstacles.

It is easy to see why we want to encourage and nurture passion in the IT organization. The growth of passion will create a widening circle of influences across the teams of IT and bring us many of the necessary elements that will carry us to the successes we must have to ensure a strong IT and a strong business. This work won't be easy, and many challenges will come our way. Passion brings us the energy, teamwork, and integrity that will help ensure success far into the future.

Reflecting for a moment on the people you have most enjoyed working with and have most admired in your career, how many of these people would you consider to be passionate? Likely, most if not all of them. Is this a simple coincidence? No way, my friends! Passion is in fact a necessary ingredient in driving the other characteristics you so admired in these people.

Passion can come to us in many ways, and we need to welcome all of these channels. First, it is likely that passion exists in some people in IT today, which is important and can be our foundation for growing more passion in the future. For the people who display passion today, their passion should be recognized and encouraged. Call attention to it both privately and publicly, and other people will take notice.

Passion has a powerful pull that brings people closer. Passion is attractive and irresistible.

The people who show passion today are great candidates for promotion, and great candidates to lead small and large teams. We want these people to be in a position to influence and lead others and we will begin to see passion grow, but we need to give it the light and air necessary to grow. Secondly, we want to evaluate any new people coming into the IT organization for passion. This should be a key quality for new transfers joining IT from other elements of the business (a more common occurrence in the future as IT becomes a more attractive organization) and for those we are interviewing for backfills or for new hires. Passion must become one of the key requirements for all hiring, right up there with the traditional priorities of experience and skills. In some cases where an organization might be struggling—lacking passion today—the quality of passion could become the top priority in hiring for some time until we have seeded the IT organization with the necessary anchors of passion for the future.

Passion must grow through intentional planning and can't be left to chance. It's just too important to not plan for and to not seek with some determination. Grow it internally, hire for it, encourage it, and recognize it. With this commitment to grow and attract passion, we will see it blossom because this is a very natural and attractive quality that only needs a few seeds. Passion is contagious, and passion is sexy. Passion is a bright light that all people are drawn to, and there will be little if any resistance once we start with only the smallest of steps. Who doesn't like passion? If we find anybody who resists, that will create an occasion for some career guidance and coaching, as all our people will need to be part of this or seek their future elsewhere. Too much is at stake to not get this right. We have talked at length about some of the desirable benefits of passion, and we should equally recognize that a lack of passion brings with it complacency, a lack of energy, slowness, hesitancy, a lack of confidence, and a natural reactiveness. Sound familiar? It should because this is very much the profile of the old, traditional IT. The IT model we must leave behind.

With this understanding of the broad and deep influences of passion, of the many wonderful things that passion brings us, we begin to appreciate that passion helps to create the soul of IT for the future; passion can help drive the transformation of IT going forward; and we simply can't create the countless good things that will touch every large and small part of IT without passion.

Finally, we should not lose sight of the simple truth that passion is wonderfully unique to humanity. The small miracle of passion can and will only come from the hearts of our people.

TEAMWORK

Sprinkled throughout the preceding pages of our book is the idea and importance of teamwork. We couldn't avoid this wonderful idea and strategy because it is so closely tied to much of the work that lies ahead of us in making IT stronger and in navigating the transformation of IT. The natural working style of IT has been that of individual domain experts working toward specific deliverables and in line with the expertise of an individual. This can be mapped to the silo-centric model that defined IT for the first thirty years of the organization. Fairly, the point could be made that teamwork has grown in the past decade, but that growth has been isolated and slower than what we must see for the future. We now call on ourselves to accelerate the evolution of teamwork in every element of IT because it brings us so much back that directly applies to the challenges that are gathering ahead of us for the business and for IT.

Remember, the common practice of IT working as individual content experts and domain masters is perfectly logical and was very much necessary due to the demands of the primary disciplines of IT and the limited staff and resources we could mobilize to complete our work and respond to the needs of the business.

In many ways this silo model was about simply surviving and wired us to not rely on the structure of a team.

While old habits are hard to break, there are times when clinging to old habits can also doom us to fail in the future. This is one such time. Meeting the growing and ever-faster-moving demands of the business can only be possible through the mobilization of small cross-functional teams. It takes a bit of time to appreciate the dynamics of small teams, but one thing we come to appreciate about the upside of working in teams is that we can in fact create much more speed, and more sustainable speed, by working in teams. These are not large and complex teams, but small cross-functional teams that can be formed and mobilized quickly with a simple and clear charter and consisting of talented and like-minded people who are focused on results.

These small cross-functional teams create a powerful engine and source of new thinking and renewal across the IT organization.

Note the choice of the words "cross-functional" in the description of these teams. This is no accident. "Cross-functional" is a vital characteristic of these teams and directly enables better performance, superior decision-making, better communications, improved transparency, faster results, and much more. Forming small teams of any composition is a good thing and certainly a big step forward, but when we form cross-functional teams versus single-function teams, well, that is another thing entirely in the best possible way. And it enables us to take a quantum leap forward.

Let's put a few numbers to these teams—a small team being something like five to eight people and cross-functional meaning approximately three to four functions across the IT organization represented on the team. Your structure might vary a bit, but this is a place to start and then adjust as needed.

The model of the cross-functional team is highly versatile and able to be productive with virtually any charter. To further enhance the characteristic of being cross-functional in nature, the size of the team also matters and enables the team to move more quickly, to be more agile, to mobilize more quickly, to finalize deliverables more quickly, to make adjustments more readily, and to communicate better. Small teams are a powerhouse and a proven model for business performance. The cross-functional composition of the team makes these awesome teams even better.

Think of this team as a group of experts brought together to drive superior results and to make each member of the team better and more productive than they can be on their own. Cross-functional teams create a natural process of checks and balances and drive better decisions. This comment on decision-making is not a casual one as better decision-making is only possible through more complete discussions, necessary debate, a broader perspective, the ability to self-govern and self-correct, and the inherent ability to validate key assumptions.

This is just the beginning of the remarkable benefits that come to life when a cross-functional team is up and running. These small cross-functional teams can be the baseline model for teamwork and always a good place to start, but there will be times when larger teams will make sense, and that is fine. Any team is better than any individual effort with only a few exceptions, and so we welcome the larger team when that is a better fit for the need. But the small cross-functional team will be the bread-and-butter for how work gets done in the future of the IT organization and becomes a new standard for productivity.

With the trust, communication, comradery, and fun that is created through teamwork, we find that this model naturally supports a better culture and the soul of the company. We are building a superior IT organization and a stronger business with this work. When we consider the words that can describe our teams at their best, including "trust" and "fun"—these get to the very heart of what we must become in the future and the results of a successful IT transformation.

Make no mistake that we can't expect to create the IT for the future without finding our character and shaping a new soul for the organization. This is a feeling that every employee carries with them every day and becomes a vital ingredient in creating the confidence, commitment, and energy that must be present to find "Great" in the world of IT. This is not possible in the absence of the organizational soul that is so human and living in our humanity and waiting to be awakened.

INTEGRITY AND HOPE

Today is connected to a better tomorrow with hope. Hope is uniquely capable of carrying us forward when challenges come, and it gives us energy and optimism when they are needed in the face of challenges and setbacks. A culture with no hope is inevitably in decline with little opportunity to find a better future.

In the tumultuous world of business today, hope is needed more than ever. So much is uncertain, there is so much change, tremendous pressures and relentless global competition in every market segment, and business is increasingly performed around the clock. The separation between work and personal has always been easy to see, but that is no longer the case. The demands of our jobs and the needs of our families have collided, and we are left to sort this out, wanting to both be successful in our roles at work and to be there for our friends and families and to somehow find time to indulge our hobbies and passions as a source of fun and fulfillment.

With all of this and more competing for our time, we are reminded of the importance of hope. We hope to get better, we hope to get smarter, we hope to be healthy and to be strong, we hope to be a better teammate, we hope to be a better spouse and friend, we hope to make our world a better place, we hope to leave a legacy, we hope to help others when they need a hand—there is no limit to where hope can take us.

The search for better begins with a desire for good, and then hope can lift us up and carry us forward.

It is fair to say that hope is hard at work bringing us little miracles every day.

A powerful partner to hope is prayer, and when we begin the journey of hope and the light that it can bring to every day, we often awaken or strengthen our faith. Regardless of your faith background and preferences, prayer is another source of tremendous good waiting to help. People who are able to incorporate hope and faith into their daily work and lives are inspirations to others, and their optimism is attractive and contagious. When there is no hope and pessimism overwhelms our thinking, the expectation of bad things to come will eclipse the hope for good things to come, and we are likely to be trapped by our own low expectations. Without hope we are pulled toward the dark things that are part of every life versus moving toward the wonderful things that bring light and happiness to our lives. This is a choice we make every day whether we consciously understand it or not. Every day is a series of small and big choices, and we should be making these choices with a plan, with a strategy to be hopeful. With that simple ideal, we see everything a little differently.

The desire for and pursuit of good and then an embrace with hope brings us a desire to be good and to do good. This carries further toward the goal that the very best people share: helping the people in our lives and shaping a better world today while influencing any way we can a better future. This brings us to Integrity.

The Oxford Dictionary defines integrity as: *the quality of being honest and having strong moral principles; moral uprightness.*

With the desire to be better in all we do and in all our relationships, the quality of integrity is inescapable. Being honest and principled, the pursuit of moral uprightness—this is a further expansion on the idea of being good and doing good and making this happen every day.

If we reflect on the ideas of hope and integrity and all they mean and all they are capable of bringing us, it becomes clear that the soul of a good company that then is capable of becoming a great company must have hope and integrity. How else can we be great for our people and for our customers? Yes, of course there are other qualities, but we highlight hope and integrity because they are often overlooked and sometimes overrun in today's frantic pace and desperate search for answers. So many people have lost sight of what should be most dear to us, what is truly important.

But there is always hope waiting to be discovered.

With the transformation of IT and the virtually limitless changes that will come and the opportunity to take a fresh look at all that we do, this is the perfect time to reassess our focus and our priorities and to redefine what we will be as an IT organization. Together, humanity is capable of anything. All that we perhaps lack today is the vision for the new IT we will become. It must be left to you, your teammates, your unique IT, and your business to define what your organization will be in the future, but hope and integrity must play a role. We will also discover—as the very best IT teams and businesses have— that a commitment to building a world-class culture and a focus on core values, including hope, integrity, and a passion for the customer, begins to change what we think and what we do every day. For what we think is important, but what we do is even more important. What we do every day will ultimately define us and will be the fabric of the perceptions formed by every person in IT and every customer we serve.

This then further forms the makeup of the soul of a company or organization of any kind that we want to be part of, that we are proud of, that we want to give our all to.

CUSTOMER SUCCESS

We conclude our discussion on the soul of the company in the only place we can, with a focus on the customer and ultimately the success our customers find through the services and products we provide. A passion for the customer and partnering with customers in working toward customer success, in however that might be defined, is critical to any successful IT culture and central to our focus on what the organization will be at its core, in its collective soul. This is everything to the IT organization seeking to be great, to be world-class.

It is possible to improve to a degree without exploring this question and without reflecting on what kind of IT we want to be in the future. Not all organizations have the desire or ability to explore this question. It's not easy, it can be painful, and it requires a level of introspection that is not natural and not comfortable. It will test us and how committed we are to this journey of IT transformation and our level of fortitude in elevating our very own IT organization to be among the very best. This journey is not unlike anything in our lives we have or may someday undertake with the goal of being extraordinary, and not just pretty good. There is a big difference. We should be honest with ourselves and with our teammates on exactly where our goals lie and the level of commitment we are willing to reach in order to meet them.

IT organizations that have reached a level of excellence and have made the necessary commitment to continuing to improve are each different to a degree, but at the same time most of them have a few things in common:

A strong culture

Natural openness to new ideas and change

Tenured staff

Defined process for innovation and acceptance of some risk-taking

Open and frequent communications

Strong team structure

A mentoring program

Recognition and celebration of success

Focus on the Customer and a direct connection to Customer feedback

This outline is consistently met with the IT organizations that are in the midst of their own transformation, have a long-term plan to perform at the highest levels, and have an understanding of the journey versus a short-term focus on projects and programs. Make no mistake, projects and their deliverables are a necessary structure for us in IT, but this work must be done in the greater context of our organizational vision and goals. This context is vital because it constantly shows us the way and ensures we have a framework for qualifying and prioritizing the daily work that occurs across the many teams of IT.

The elements shown above contribute to building the right feeling in the IT organization, a bit of swagger, an organization our people want to be part of and want to stay with far into the future. Yes, these things and more make up the character and soul of IT and make the teams and the overall organization something special.

I have had the good fortune of witnessing the transformation of some of the leading global IT organizations today, which consistently align around a pattern of thinking and behavior that codifies success at every level. We can think of this as a lifestyle change and it calls us to see everything differently. In the process of making these changes, we are training our teams to think a certain way; to work through a decision-making and problem-solving process is everything we do, so we are training our people to find the right outcome in virtually any circumstance. Good decision-making is a trained skill, and enabled only with a disciplined and consistent approach.

What does this have to do with customer success? Everything. There should always be a few final questions we ask ourselves when making the many decisions that are required across IT every day, and of confirming our priorities when allocating precious time and resources to the work that drives IT.

In asking these questions of ourselves and using these questions to drive the necessary discussion and debate, we can't get too far off track:

> *How does this decision impact our customers?*

> *What would our customers say if they were at the table with us?*

> *Is this decision true to our customer success core value?*

> *Does this action violate any commitments we have made to customers?*

This should be a simple discussion and enable our teams to get to the heart of the matter very quickly. Normally, it is easy to evaluate if our actions are in line with customer success or not. If not, the people of IT need to push back and speak up quickly so the necessary adjustments can be made.

This is a reminder that a commitment to customer success is not just a poster we put in the lunch room, not just a slogan the marketing team creates.

Customer success is a lifestyle we live, one that is enforced through the many large and small decisions we make every day.

In staying true to the principles outlined in the chapter, we are forming the character, the soul of IT, and it becomes natural for us. A good habit has been formed at every level of the organization through training and reinforcement, and it becomes how we think and how we act.

The soul of IT is alive and well and living in every person today and quickly embraced by any new people who join the team tomorrow and far into the future.

FINAL THOUGHTS

I hope you have enjoyed exploring the humanity of IT as much as I have enjoyed bringing a few ideas to light through the pages of this book. To my knowledge, very little has been published that focuses on the wonderful people of IT and no books that have been dedicated to this fascinating topic of the simple humanity of IT, one that has been overlooked for far too long. To an extent this all makes perfect sense because the IT organization has a natural affinity for technology—we certainly love our tools, applications, and systems—and because the business tends to see IT as those smart ladies and gentlemen who are all about technology and assets and data, our people continue to be pushed aside. But we should expect to see a recalibration of the identity of the IT organization and with this a new understanding and appreciation of the people who make all that is good happen in the IT organization every day.

The professionals of IT are surrounded with high expectations. When everything in the business is working as it should, the infrastructure of IT is invisible and very much taken for granted. The business assumes everything should work, regardless of how demanding and challenging that might be given the complexities of today's global markets and the always-on lifestyle we increasingly live. This expectation is fair. However, when something we rely on to do our jobs every day is not working—think email, our mobile phone, or Internet access for example—then the IT organization comes into focus instantly. All eyes turn to our teams, and we find that customers and employees frantically await a return to normal service, and with this life is good once again. While this focus on the people of IT often only occurs when something is wrong, we are reminded of just how much we need these talented people. When we need them, we *really* need them.

Although it does not happen nearly enough, when we do take the time to look more closely at the makeup of IT and the rhythms and substance of the vital work that occurs every day, we begin to appreciate the remarkable abilities of our people, the wonderful human element of every IT organization. The intent of the book is simply to bring more attention to the hardworking and underappreciated people toiling tirelessly behind the scenes and expecting very little in return. But we owe them much more than we have perhaps been able to provide in the past. And that all begins with understanding and then appreciation that can grow into thoughtful support of these teams and planning for a very different future. The current trajectory of IT will change over the next decade and for some organizations is changing now. What we will discover is that the transformation of IT is very real, is upon us today, but holds a few surprises—not the least of which being that the transformation is not solely about exciting new technologies, including AI and automation, as many have assumed. We must come to appreciate there is a more critical element of this transformation, and that is connected to our people. The heart and soul of the IT organization live here, in our people. Young and old, new and experienced, people of every background with very different lives and wonderfully diverse skills and beliefs. This is the future of IT and the key to a stronger, more dynamic, more innovative, more assertive team, better able to lead and deliver value into a future that will only see the business succeed as far as IT and the people of IT are able to take us. Yes, of course some will argue the point, and some will think this view is nothing less than crazy thinking, but I'm confident this new business landscape will come to pass in the next decade. And the secret will be found in the most unlikely of places—within the wondrous people of the business and beginning with the people of IT representing a virtually unlimited upside.

The signs of this remarkable and unexpected shift are there, if only we slow down and take a thoughtful look at the evolving influences that are happening today in every business. This future will find more of the superstars in the business working in IT, creative and strong compensation plans for the same people, the IT organization as a desirable destination for a new generation of worker, and a deeper understanding of the value uniquely provided by the workforce of IT.

All of this and much more is the backdrop against which I wrote this book on the Humanity of IT, and all written with admiration and wonder. With the book now completed, I have no doubt the appreciation for the people of IT will come to new light in the years ahead, and the long overdue attention will come to these same people and result in new, challenging, and rewarding careers in IT and a future generation of leadership that will put IT into good hands for decades to come. These advancements and improvements will make the IT organization itself stronger no doubt, but will equally improve every element of the business and will be a key differentiator for the new generation of market leaders in every industry and in every center of business around the world.

I look forward to hearing your stories when our paths cross in the future. Keep the faith, my friends.

Kevin
@kevinjsmith4IT

REFERENCES

The IT Imperative. Kevin J. Smith. The Anima Group, 2018.

One IT, One Business. Kevin J. Smith. The Anima Group, 2019.

NOTES

_____

_____

_____

_____

_____

_____

_____

_____

_____

_____

_____

_____

_____

_____

_____

_____

_____

_____

_____

NOTES

NOTES

NOTES

NOTES

_____
_____
_____
_____
_____
_____
_____
_____
_____
_____
_____
_____
_____
_____
_____
_____
_____
_____
_____

NOTES

NOTES

NOTES

NOTES

NOTES

NOTES

NOTES

NOTES

NOTES

NOTES

NOTES

_____

_____

_____

_____

_____

_____

_____

_____

_____

_____

_____

_____

_____

_____

_____

_____

_____

_____

_____

_____

NOTES

NOTES

NOTES

NOTES

NOTES

NOTES

NOTES

NOTES

NOTES

NOTES

www.ingramcontent.com/pod-product-compliance
Lightning Source LLC
Chambersburg PA
CBHW051230050326
40689CB00007B/870